Partners
Praise

First published in 1979
by
Stainer and Bell Ltd
and
Chester House Publications
on behalf of
The Methodist Church
Division of Education and Youth

ISBN 0 85249 554 4

EDITED

BY

FRED PRATT GREEN

AND

BERNARD BRALEY

GALLIARD   CHESTER HOUSE PUBLICATIONS

Printed in Great Britain by Galliard (Printers) Ltd

Great Yarmouth

CONTENTS

PREFACE

WHEN YOUNG AND OLD COME TO CHURCH TOGETHER

This book tackles a dilemma of all who lead such services. How do we prepare so that the event is not an occasion for adults with children looking on or for children with adults on the sideline?

Sunday services include the twin elements of worship and learning. Hymns play a major role in both. Here we seek to include material especially suitable for each age group which is acceptable in some measure to all others. The childlike is acceptable to the adult; growth in understanding by a child involves grappling with some ideas and language which will not be fully understood.

THE GREAT HYMNS FROM THE CENTURIES

A major part of a full diet of hymnody comes from the rich heritage it is the privilege of present-day Christians to enjoy. There are however difficulties where words have changed their meanings or where imagery used is now outside common experience. But usually these drawbacks are outweighed by the experience that we are part of a worshipping community at one with Christians of every age and place. Insights given to Christian believers over many centuries are a necessary balance to be set alongside the theological emphasis of a particular time and place.

THE CONTRIBUTION OF CONTEMPORARY CHRISTIANS

None the less, our role is to serve the present age. To omit from our worship the insights and creativity of recent writing would be to deprive worshippers of the chance of enjoying a rich harvest of words and music in praise of God. Some hymns and songs will not survive the limited life-span of this kind of book. Others will be passed on to future generations as the particular insights of our times. The Joint Editors hope too that the book will encourage contemporary writers to put into hymn and song what the theologians are discerning may be the special contribution of this last part of the twentieth century.

THE DIVERSITY OF MUSIC

The General Editors have encouraged the Music Editors to use music of many styles in this collection.

AIDS TO WORSHIP AND LEARNING

There are many aids which can properly be employed within worship. For example we would encourage leaders of worship sometimes to give congregations time to read hymns before or after singing them, to ask musicians to pause sometimes between verses, to highlight the Biblical sources of particular parts of the text, to tell the stories that inspired their writing and how they have been useful in the past. Some hymns lend themselves to visual illustration in mime and drama, others are especially suitable as setting the scene for action within the Liturgy.

GAINING THE BEST FROM THIS BOOK

Avoid only using those hymns you like best. Others with different tastes will be at worship too. We all grow by using that which does not immediately appeal. The book is arranged in broad sections and at the beginning of each is a list of hymns from standard books commended for use alongside the hymns and songs printed in Partners in Praise.

The Music Edition contains extensive Theme Indexes to help leaders of worship.

TEAM WORK

The Joint Editors acknowledge their debt to the Joint Music Editors, Dr Allen Percival, CBE, until recently Principal of the Guildhall School of Music and Drama, and Rev. T. Brian Coleman and to the members of their Advisory Group: Rev. Martin V. Caldwell, Mr Philip L. Carter, Dr. Byron Evans, Rev. John M. Marsh, Rev. Barry Miller, Mrs Ida Prins-Buttle, Rev. Peter D. Smith and Mr Ian Wragg. They also gratefully acknowledge the help of the Secretary of the Advisory Committee, Rev. Gordon Turner.

COPYRIGHT

The Joint Editors regret that a small number of hymns they would have wished to include have been denied them by the copyright owners or have been too expensive in fees for inclusion. Generally however, they are grateful for the ready response of all owners of copyright and believe all have been properly consulted and acknowledged. If there have been any unintentional oversights, they would be grateful to have them drawn to their notice.

Fred Pratt Green

Bernard Braley

1979

APPROACH

TO

WORSHIP

**in which we praise God,
rejoice in his creation
and undertake to care for it.**

Recommended hymns from standard books

S1 All creatures of our God and King
S2 All people that on earth do dwell
S3 All things bright and beautiful
S4 Awake, my soul, and with the sun
S5 Christ whose glory fills the skies
S6 Fill thou my life, O Lord my God
S7 For the beauty of the earth
S8 From all that dwell below the skies
S9 I sing the almighty power of God
S10 King of glory, King of peace
S11 Let all the world in every corner sing
S12 Lift up your hearts! We lift them, Lord, to thee
S13 Lord God, by whom all change is wrought
S14 Now thank we all our God
S15 O Lord of every lovely thing
S16 O Lord of life, thy quickening voice
S17 O worship the King
S18 Praise, my soul, the King of heaven
S19 Praise the Lord who reigns above
S20 Praise the Lord! Ye heavens, adore him
S21 Praise to the living God
S22 Praise to the Lord, the Almighty, the King of creation
S23 The spacious firmament on high
S24 We plough the fields, and scatter
S25 Ye servants of God

1 SONG OF THE CHRISTIANS

1 There are songs for us all to sing —
Sing them loud and clear:
Songs of joy and hope and peace,
Of courage and good cheer.
As the love of the Lord floods our hearts,
This is where our worship starts:
With the song of praise Creation sings
To all with ears to hear.

2 There's a song for us all to sing —
Sing it loud and clear:
It's the gospel song we sing
All seasons of the year:
How the Word became flesh for our sakes;
Of the difference Easter makes:
It's the song of joy we Christians sing
To all with ears to hear.

3 There's a song for us all to sing —
Sing it loud and clear:
It's the song we sinners sing
As the Lord of life draws near:
When the sheep that is lost will be found,
And the son is homeward bound:
It's the song of hope we Christians sing
To all with ears to hear.

4 There's a song for us all to sing —
Sing it loud and clear:
It's the song we are bold to sing
Of the love that casts out fear:
Of the Spirit who makes us all one;
And of freedoms to be won:
It's the song of peace we Christians sing
To all with ears to hear.

Fred Pratt Green (1903–)

2 MAGNIFICAT

1 Tell out, my soul, the greatness of the
  Lord!
Unnumbered blessings, give my spirit
  voice:
Tender to me the promise of his Word;
In God my Saviour shall my heart rejoice.

2 Tell out, my soul, the greatness of his
  name!
Make known his might, the deeds his arm
  has done;

His mercy sure, from age to age the same;
His holy name — the Lord, the Mighty One.

3 Tell out, my soul, the greatness of his might!
Powers and dominions lay their glory by.
Proud hearts and stubborn wills are put to flight,
The hungry fed, the humble lifted high.

4 Tell out, my soul, the glories of his Word!
Firm in his promise, and his mercy sure.
Tell out, my soul, the greatness of the Lord
To children's children and for evermore!

Timothy Dudley-Smith (1926–)

3 INVITATION TO WORSHIP

1 Come and join us,
Come and join us
As we celebrate in worship.
Come and join us,
Come and join us,
Come and join us all today.

Peter D. Smith (1938–)

4 THANK YOU!

1 Thank you for every new good morning,
Thank you for every fresh new day,
Thank you that I may cast my burdens
Wholly on to thee.

2 Thank you for every friend I have, Lord,
Thank you for everyone I know,
Thank you when I can feel forgiveness
To my greatest foe.

3 Thank you for leisure and employment,
Thank you for every heartfelt joy,
Thank you for all that makes me happy
And for melody.

4 Thank you for every shade and sorrow,
Thank you for comfort in your Word,
Thank you that I am guided by you
Everywhere I go.

5 Thank you for grace to know your Gospel,
Thank you for all your Spirit's power,
Thank you for your unfailing love
Which reaches far and near.

6 Thank you for free and full salvation,
Thank you for grace to hold it fast,
Thank you, O Lord, I want to thank you
That I'm free to thank.

Martin G. Schneider (1930–)
English words by M.A. Baughen (1930–)

5 JOY, PEACE, LOVE

1 Give me joy in my heart, keep me praising,
Give me joy in my heart, I pray;
Give me joy in my heart, keep me praising,
Keep me praising till the break of day:
Sing Hosanna! Sing Hosanna!
Sing Hosanna to the King of kings!
Sing Hosanna! Sing Hosanna!
Sing Hosanna to the King.

2 Give me peace in my heart, keep me loving,
Give me peace in my heart, I pray;
Give me peace in my heart, keep me loving,
Keep me loving till the break of day:
CHORUS

3 Give me love in my heart, keep me serving,
Give me love in my heart, I pray;
Give me love in my heart, keep me serving,
Keep me serving till the break of day:
CHORUS

Traditional

6 SHOUT FOR JOY!

O Lord! Shout for joy!
O Lord! Shout for joy!

1 All together shout for joy!
All together shout for joy!
CHORUS

2 God is good so shout for joy!
God is good so shout for joy!
CHORUS

3 Let us praise him! Shout for joy!
In our worship, shout for joy!
CHORUS

4 Clap and sing and shout for joy!
Dance and sing and shout for joy!
CHORUS

Negro spiritual adapted Peter D. Smith (1938–)

7 PRAISE EVERY MORNING

1 Morning has broken
  Like the first morning,
  Blackbird has spoken
  Like the first bird.
  Praise for the singing!
  Praise for the morning!
  Praise for them, springing
  Fresh from the Word!

2 Sweet the rain's new fall
  Sunlit from heaven,
  Like the first dewfall
  On the first grass.
  Praise for the sweetness
  Of the wet garden,
  Sprung in completeness
  Where his feet pass.

3 Mine is the sunlight!
  Mine is the morning!
  Born of the one light
  Eden saw play!
  Praise with elation,
  Praise every morning
  God's new creation
  Of the new day!

Eleanor Farjeon (1881-1965)

8 BREAD FOR THE WORLD

1 Praise and thanksgiving,
  Father, we offer
  For all things living
  Thou madest good.
  Harvest of sown fields,
  Fruits of the orchard,
  Hay from the mown fields,
  Blossom and wood.

2 Bless thou the labour
  We bring to serve thee,
  That with our neighbour
  We may be fed.
  Sowing or tilling
  We would work with thee,
  Harvesting, milling,
  For daily bread.

3 Father, providing
  Food for thy children,
  Thy wisdom guiding
  Teaches us share
  One with another,
  So that, rejoicing
  With us, our brother
  May know thy care.

4 Then will thy blessing
  Reach every people,
  All men confessing
  Thy gracious hand.
  Where thy will reigneth
  No man will hunger —
  Thy love sustaineth;
  Fruitful the land.

Albert F. Bayly (1901–)

9 PRAYING AND PRAISING

1 Praise to God in the highest! Bless us O
    Father:
  Praise to thee!

2 Guide and prosper the nations, rulers and
    people:
  Praise to thee!

3 May the truth in its beauty flourish
    triumphant:
  Praise to thee!

4 May the mills bring us bread, for food and
    for giving:
  Praise to thee!

5 May the good be obeyed and evil be
    conquered:
  Praise to thee!

6 Give us laughter and set us gaily rejoicing:
  Praise to thee!

7 Peace on earth and goodwill be ever among us
  Praise to thee!

Traditional Russian translated AFD

10 THE SONG OF CAEDMON

1 Oh praise him! Oh praise him! Oh praise
    him!
  Oh praise him! Oh praise him! Oh praise
    him!

He made the heavens, he made our sky,
The sun, the moon, the stars on high.
He formed our world, his mighty hand
Divided sea and land.
He moves in wind and rain and snow,
His life is in all things that grow.
Oh praise him!
Oh praise him!
Oh praise him!

2 Oh praise him! Oh praise him! Oh praise
   him!
   Oh praise him! Oh praise him! Oh praise
   him!
   His joy is in the eagle's flight,
   The tiger's roar, the lion's might,
   The lamb, the python and the whale,
   The spider, ant and snail.
   All things that leap and swim and fly
   On land and sea and in the sky,
   They praise him,
   They praise him,
   They praise him.

3 Oh praise him! Oh praise him! Oh praise
   him!
   Oh praise him! Oh praise him! Oh praise
   him!
   He lives his life in love and joy,
   In man and woman, girl and boy.
   His purpose is in me and you,
   In what we are and do.
   His love is in us when we sing
   With every God-created thing,
   And praise him,
   And praise him,
   And praise him!

Arthur Scholey (1932–)

11 SONG OF GLADNESS

1 I hurl up my gladness
   Like birds towards heaven,
   I hear the sweet music
   Creation is singing,
   The rocks are all ringing
   Awaking the sleeping
   With songs of all living
   That live beyond dying.
   All things are united in God.
   I hurl up my gladness
   Like birds towards heaven.

2 My joy is with Jesus
   Who dwells in my being.
   The Maker of all things
   Was born in a stable.
   He gave us his loving
   Upon a cross dying.
   His wounded love seeks us
   Through sorrow and darkness
   And none is forgotten by God.
   I hurl up my gladness
   Like birds towards heaven.

3 I've joy in the power
   Of God's Holy Spirit,
   The deep murmuring waters
   Like words beyond speaking.
   One cup is for all men
   And shared by all nations.
   They know the same gladness,
   They feel the same sadness,
   All men are united in God.
   I hurl up my gladness
   Like birds towards heaven.

*Adapted by Peter D. Smith (1938–) and
Chris Rogers (1922–) from Swedish of
Anders Frostenson (1906–)*

12 ALL KINDS OF LIGHT

1 Father, we thank you.
   For the light that shines all the day;
   For the bright sky you have given,
   Most like your heaven;
   Father, we thank you.

2 Father, we thank you.
   For the lamps that lighten the way;
   For human skill's exploration
   Of your creation;
   Father, we thank you.

3 Father, we thank you.
   For the friends who brighten our play;
   For your command to call others
   Sisters and brothers;
   Father, we thank you.

4 Father, we thank you.
   For your love in Jesus today,
   Giving us hope for tomorrow
   Through joy and sorrow;
   Father, we thank you.

Caryl Micklem (1925–)

13 THE LORDSHIP OF CHRIST

1 Alleluia! Alleluia! Alleluia!
  In Christ we join to sing with praise
  His Lordship over all our days,
  His grace to order all our ways.
  Alleluia!

2 In Christ we come ourselves to share,
  Each others' pains we gladly bear,
  Each one of us within his care,
  Alleluia!

3 To share the self beneath the mask,
  To share each God-appointed task,
  Christ's strength in prayer for all to ask,
  Alleluia!

4 To dance with joy, to weep in grief,
  To search and find a true belief
  Beneath Christ's careful watching brief,
  Alleluia!

5 To Christ the Lord of all our days,
  To Christ the Lord of all our ways,
  Let Christians sing in humble praise,
  Alleluia!

Bernard Braley (1924–)

14 THE GRANDEUR OF GOD

1 Sing of the grandeur which is God
  Beyond where mortal minds can reach,
  The more we search Creation's law
  The more we find he has to teach.

2 Sing of the parenthood of God
  Who knows each strand of human hair,
  A God whose grandeur yet permits
  For each his individual care.

3 Sing of the childlikeness of God
  Delighting in each new born day,
  A deeply caring God who knows
  The dancelike holiness of play.

4 Sing of the energy of God
  Which activates yet does not tire,
  The source of Nature's light and heat,
  The driving force of prophets' fire.

5 Sing of the life force which is God,
  The spring of every living breath,
  The ground on which our being rests,
  The joy of life past human death.

Bernard Braley (1924–)

15 CREATOR SPIRIT

1 Fire is lighting torch and lamp at night;
  Fire outbursts into power and light.
  Come, O God, Creator, Spirit, now
  Fill all our lives with your fire.

2 Wind is battering waves of sea on land;
  Wind is grinding the rocks to sand.
  Come, O God, Creator, Spirit, now
  Order anew all your world.

3 Water gushes down the cleft of space;
  Living water and spring of grace.
  Come, O God, Creator, Spirit, now
  Grant us your life and your light.

John B. Geyer (1932–)

16 EVERYTHING IS HIS

1 For the fruits of his creation,
  Thanks be to God;
  For his gifts to every nation,
  Thanks be to God:
  For the ploughing, sowing, reaping,
  Silent growth while we are sleeping,
  Future needs in earth's safe keeping,
  Thanks be to God.

2 In the just reward of labour,
  God's will is done;
  In the help we give our neighbour,
  God's will is done:
  In our world-wide task of caring
  For the hungry and despairing,
  In the harvests we are sharing,
  God's will is done.

3 For the harvests of his Spirit,
  Thanks be to God;
  For the good we all inherit,
  Thanks be to God:
  For the wonders that astound us,
  For all truths that still confound us,
  Most of all that love has found us,
  Thanks be to God.

Fred Pratt Green (1903–)

17 GOD'S FARM

1 God, whose farm is all Creation,
   Take the gratitude we give;
   Take the finest of our harvest,
   Crops we grow that men may live.

2 Take our ploughing, seeding, reaping,
   Hopes and fears of sun and rain,
   All our thinking, planning, waiting,
   Ripened in this fruit and grain.

3 All our labour, all our watching,
   All our calendar of care,
   In these crops of your creation,
   Take, O God: they are our prayer.

John Arlott (1914–)

18 SEEING, HEARING, TOUCHING

1 Give to us eyes
   That we may truly see
   Flight of a bird,
   The shapes in a tree,
   Curve of a hillside,
   Colours in a stone.
   Give to us seeing eyes, O Lord.

2 Give to us ears
   That we may truly hear
   Music in birdsong,
   Rippling water clear,
   Whine of the winter wind,
   Laughter of a friend.
   Give to us hearing ears, O Lord.

3 Give to us hands
   That we may truly know
   Patterns in tree bark,
   Crispness of the snow,
   Smooth feel of velvet,
   Shapes in a shell.
   Give to us knowing hands, O Lord.

*Peggy Blakeley (1921–) and
Don Harper (1921–)*

19 FEEDING THE FAMILY

1 Earth takes the seed,
   Makes food for you and me,
   We take the food
   To feed a family.

2 Earth and the seed
   Need sun and rain and care,
   So we give thanks
   In learning how to share.

Anthony Geering (1943–)

20 THE LAUGHTER OF THE LORD

1 Bread is the laughter of the man in the
     field,
   Books are the laughter of the wise,
   *Love is the laughter of the man who walks
     with God,*
   Love is the laughter of the Lord.

2 Fish are the laughter of the man in his
     boat,
   Lambs are his laughter in the hills,
   CHORUS

3 Birds are the laughter of the man in the
     wood,
   Songs are the laughter of his soul,
   CHORUS

4 A child is the laughter of the mother in her
     home,
   Friends are the laughter of her child,
   CHORUS

Marian Collihole (1933–)

21 THE STEWARDSHIP OF EARTH

1 God in his love for us lent us this planet,
   Gave it a purpose in time and in space:
   Small as a spark from the fire of creation,
   Cradle of life and the home of our race.

2 Thanks be to God for its bounty and
     beauty,
   Life that sustains us in body and mind:
   Plenty for all, if we learn how to share it,
   Riches undreamed of to fathom and find.

3 Long have the wars of man ruined its
     harvest;
   Long has earth bowed to the terror of
     force;
   Long have we wasted what others have
     need of,
   Poisoned the fountain of life at its source.

4 Earth is the Lord's: it is ours to enjoy it,
Ours, as his stewards, to farm and defend.
From its pollution, misuse, and
destruction,
Good Lord deliver us, world without end!

Fred Pratt Green (1903–)

22 OUR STEWARDSHIP AND BRIEF

1 The earth, the sky, the oceans
And all that they contain;
The world with all its secrets,
It is the Lord's domain.
To rule his great Creation,
God has endowed mankind
With gifts of strength and courage
And an inventive mind.

2 To us from birth is given
Our stewardship and brief;
To search for truth and purpose,
To find the heart of life.
God calls us to adventure
With work of hand and brain;
To share with all his people
The profits we may gain.

3 For quest and exploration,
Our God has given the key
To free the hidden forces
And wealth of soil and sea.
To new advance in science,
Research to conquer pain,
To growth in skill and knowledge
We are by God ordained.

4 We pledge ourselves to service,
That with the help of Christ
We may be able stewards
Of all that does exist.
Whate'er we may discover,
On earth, in outer space,
God grant that we may use it
To bless the human race.

Fred Kaan (1929–)

23 MAKING AND MENDING

1 Our God is one who makes things.
All life in earth or star
Is there because he wakes things
And makes them what they are.
So often we mistake things
And mix up bad and good,
And then we spoil and break things
And feel misunderstood.

2 We all can learn to make things
If that is what we want,
Perhaps to sew or bake things,
Perhaps to build or plant.
It's easier to break things,
But when we've once begun
With hands and minds to make things,
It's hard but much more fun.

3 God's Spirit works to shake things
Until at last we see
How sadly we mistake things,
How different life could be.
We need not spoil or break things,
Let's build and not destroy.
We'll work with God to make things
And share our Maker's joy.

Rosamond Herklots (1905–)

24 USING OUR GIFTS

1 Come to us, creative Spirit,
In our Father's house,
Every natural talent foster,
Hidden skills arouse,
That within your earthly temple
Wise and simple
May rejoice.

2 Poet, painter, music-maker,
All your treasures bring;
Craftsman, actor, graceful dancer,
Make your offering:
Join your hands in celebration!
Let Creation
Shout and sing!

3 Word from God Eternal springing
Fill our minds, we pray,
And in all artistic vision
Give integrity.
May the flame within us burning
Kindle yearning
Day by day.

4 In all places and forever
Glory be expressed
To the Son, with God the Father,
And the Spirit blest.
In our worship and our living
Keep us striving
Towards the best.

David Mowbray (1938–)

25 IN GOD'S HANDS

The line of each verse is sung four times

1 He's got the whole world in his hands.

2 He's got the wind and the rain in his hands.

3 He's got you and me, brother, in his hands.

4 He's got the little tiny baby in his hands.

5 He's got the whole Church in his hands.

Traditional

26 THE RENEWAL OF EARTH

1 Thank you, Lord, for water, soil and air —
Large gifts supporting everything that
lives.
Forgive our spoiling and abuse of them.
Help us renew the face of the earth,
Help us renew the face of the earth.

2 Thank you, Lord, for minerals and ores —
The basis of all building, wealth and speed.
Forgive our reckless plundering and waste.
Help us renew the face of the earth,
Help us renew the face of the earth.

3 Thank you, Lord, for priceless energy —
Stored in each atom, gathered from the
sun.
Forgive our greed and carelessness of
power.
Help us renew the face of the earth,
Help us renew the face of the earth.

4 Thank you, Lord, for weaving Nature's
life
Into a seamless robe, a fragile whole.
Forgive our haste, that tampers unawares.
Help us renew the face of the earth,
Help us renew the face of the earth.

5 Thank you, Lord, for making planet Earth
A home for us and ages yet unborn.
Help us to share, consider, save and store.
Come and renew the face of the earth,
Come and renew the face of the earth.

Brian A. Wren (1936–)

27 SHARING THE HARVEST

1 Now join we, to praise the Creator,
Our voices in worship and song;
We stand to recall with thanksgiving
That to him all seasons belong.
We thank you, O God, for your goodness,
For the joy and abundance of crops,
For food that is stored in our larders,
For all we can buy in the shops.

2 But also of need and starvation
We sing with concern and despair,
Of skills that are used for destruction,
Of land that is burnt and laid bare.
We cry for the plight of the hungry
Whilst harvests are left on the field,
For orchards neglected and wasting,
For produce from markets withheld.

3 The song grows in depth and in wideness;
The earth and its people are one,
There can be no thanks without giving,
No words without deeds that are done.
Then teach us, O Lord of the harvest,
To be humble in all that we claim;
To share what we have with the nations,
To care for the world in your name.

Fred Kaan (1929–)

28 A NEW SONG

1 Sing a new song to the Lord,
He to whom wonders belong!
Rejoice in his triumph and tell of his
power —
O sing to the Lord a new song!

2 Now to the end of the earth
See his salvation is shown:
And still he remembers his mercy and
truth,
Unchanging in love to his own.

3 Sing a new song and rejoice,
Publish his praises abroad!
Let voices in chorus, with trumpet and
horn,
Resound for the joy in the Lord!

4 Join with the hills and the sea
Thunders of praise to prolong!
In judgement and justice he comes to the
Earth —
O sing to the Lord a new song!

Timothy Dudley-Smith (1926–)

THE LORD JESUS

**in which we sing of
the birth, life, death and
resurrection of Jesus Christ.**

Recommended hymns from standard books

BIRTH (in addition to well-known carols)

S26 Earth hath many a noble city
S27 Glory be to God on high
S28 God from on high hath heard
S29 Hark the glad sound! The Saviour comes
S30 Let earth and heaven combine
S31 Love came down at Christmas
S32 O come, O come, Immanuel
S33 Of the Father's love begotten
S34 Songs of praise the angels sang
S35 Stupendous height of heavenly love
S36 The Maker of the sun and moon
S37 The race that long in darkness pined

LIFE (see also CHRIST AND OUR DISCIPLESHIP)

S38 All praise to thee for thou O King divine
S39 A man there lived in Galilee
S40 At even, ere the sun was set
S41 Hail to the Lord who comes
S42 My song is love unknown
S43 O Jesus, King most wonderful
S44 O love, how deep, how broad, how high
S45 Thou didst leave thy throne
S46 Ye neighbours and friends of Jesus draw near

DEATH AND RESURRECTION

S47 Ah, holy Jesu, how hast thou offended
S48 All glory, laud and honour
S49 At the Cross, her station keeping
S50 Away with gloom, away with doubt
S51 Beneath the Cross of Jesus
S52 Christ the Lord is risen today
S53 Come, ye faithful, raise the strain
S54 Good Christian men, rejoice and sing
S55 Hail the day that sees him rise
S56 Hail, thou once despised Jesus
S57 I know that my Redeemer lives
S58 In the Cross of Christ I glory
S59 On wings of living light
S60 O sacred Head once wounded
S61 Praise to the Holiest in the height
S62 Ride on, ride on in majesty
S63 Sing, my tongue, the glorious battle
S64 Sing we triumphant hymns of praise
S65 The day of Resurrection!
S66 The head that once was crowned with thorns
S67 There is a green hill far away
S68 The strife is o'er, the battle done
S69 Thine be the glory, risen, conquering Son
S70 Welcome, happy morning! Age to age shall say
S71 When I survey the wondrous Cross

29 ADVENT SONG

1 Long ago, prophets knew
  Christ would come, born a Jew,
  Come to make all things new;
  Bear his People's burden,
  Freely love and pardon.
  Ring, bells, ring, ring, ring!
  Sing, choirs, sing, sing, sing!
  When he comes,
  When he comes,
  Who will make him welcome?

2 God in time, God in man,
  This is God's timeless plan:
  He will come, as a man,
  Born himself of woman,
  God divinely human.
  CHORUS

3 Mary hail! Though afraid,
  She believed, she obeyed.
  In her womb, God is laid;
  Till the time expected,
  Nurtured and protected.
  CHORUS

4 Journey ends! Where afar
  Bethl'em shines, like a star,
  Stable door stands ajar.
  Unborn Son of Mary,
  Saviour, do not tarry!
  CHORUS

Fred Pratt Green (1903–)

30 GOD IS LOVE

1 God is Love: his the care,
  Tending each, everywhere.
  God is Love — all is there!
  Jesus came to show him,
  That mankind might know him:
  Sing aloud, loud, loud!
  Sing aloud, loud, loud!
  God is good!
  God is Truth! God is Beauty! Praise him!

2 None can see God above;
  All have here man to love;
  Thus may we Godward move
  Finding him in others,
  Holding all men brothers:
  CHORUS

3 Jesus lived here for men,
   Strove and died, rose again,
   Rules our hearts, now as then;
   For he came to save us
   By the truth he gave us:
   CHORUS

4 To our Lord praise we sing —
   Light and life, friend and king,
   Coming down love to bring.
   Pattern for our duty,
   Showing God in beauty:
   CHORUS

Percy Dearmer (1867-1936)

31 KING OF KINGS YET BORN OF MARY

1 Let all mortal flesh keep silence,
   And with fear and trembling stand;
   Ponder nothing earthly-minded,
   For with blessing in his hand
   Christ our God to earth desendeth,
   Our full homage to demand.

2 King of kings, yet born of Mary,
   As of old on earth he stood,
   Lord of lords, in human vesture —
   In the body and the blood —
   He will give to all the faithful
   His own self for heav'nly food.

3 Rank on rank the host of heaven
   Spreads its vanguard on the way,
   As the Light of Light descendeth
   From the realms of endless day,
   That the powers of hell may vanish
   As the darkness clears away.

4 At his feet the six-winged seraph;
   Cherubim with sleepless eye
   Veil their faces to the Presence,
   As with ceaseless voice they cry —
   Alleluia, Alleluia,
   Alleluia, Lord most high!

Liturgy of St James translated by
G. Moultrie (1829-1885)

32 THE UNIQUENESS OF CHRIST

1 Christ is the world's Light, he and none
      other;
   Born in our darkness, he became our
      Brother.

If we have seen him, we have seen the
      Father:
   Glory to God on high.

2 Christ is the world's Peace, he and none
      other;
   No man can serve him and despise his
      brother.
   Who else unites us, one in God the Father?
   Glory to God on high.

3 Christ is the world's Life, he and none other
   Sold once for silver, murdered here, our
      Brother —
   He, who redeems us, reigns with God the
      Father:
   Glory to God on high.

4 Give God the glory, God and none other;
   Give God the glory, Spirit, Son and Father;
   Give God the glory, God in man my
      brother;
   Glory to God on high.

Fred Pratt Green (1903–)

33 WHICH ONE IS WHICH

1 I come like a beggar
   With a gift in my hand;
   I come like a beggar
   With a gift in my hand.
   By the hungry I will feed you,
   By the poor I make you rich,
   By the broken I will mend you.
   Tell me,
   Which one is which?

2 I come like a prisoner
   To bring you the key,
   I come like a prisoner
   To bring you the key:
   CHORUS

3 By the need of another,
   By the gift that I bring;
   By the need of another,
   By the gift that I bring.
   CHORUS

Sydney Carter (1915–)

34 ANOTHER DAY

*This Advent song is included to enable
children to respond to the idea of waiting*

1 Darkness of the night brings us to the morn,
Rising sun of light tells the day is born.
Rejoice all people of the Earth,
Rejoice in life, rejoice in birth,
Another day.

2 Brightness of the light wakes us from our
      sleep,
Brings again the day, time its pattern
      keeps.
Rejoice all people of the Earth,
Rejoice in life, rejoice in birth,
Another day.

John Tearnan (1937–)

35 ADVENT ACROSTIC

1 A is for Advent:
Season of joy,
Jesus is coming;
Worship this wonderful boy.

2 D for Deliverer:
Fighting the wrong,
Jesus the Saviour;
Join in a welcoming song.

3 V for his Visit:
Banishing night,
Jesus the Day-star,
Candles of love are alight.

4 E for Excitement:
Yes, he will come,
Jesus expected,
Open your hearts to God's son.

5 N for his Nearness:
Comforting arm,
Jesus our brother,
Keeping his children from harm.

6 T for his Triumph:
Triumph of right,
Jesus is reigning,
Trust in his conquering might

Cyril G. Hambly (1931–)

36 ADVENT CANDLES

1 The holly and the ivy
Are dancing in a ring,
Round the berry-bright red candles
And the white and shining King.

2 Oh, one is for the prophets
And for the light they bring.
They are candles in the darkness,
All alight for Christ the King.

3 And two for John the Baptist.
He calls on us to sing:
'O prepare the way for Jesus Christ,
He is coming, Christ the King.'

4 And three for Mother Mary.
'I cannot see the way,
But you promise me a baby.
I believe you. I obey.'

5 And four are for God's people
In every age and day.
We are watching for his coming.
We believe and we obey.

6 And Christ is in the centre,
For this is his birthday,
With the shining nights of Christmas
Singing, 'He has come today.'

Emily Chisholm (1910–)

37 HERE WE GO UP TO BETHLEHEM

1 Here we go up to Bethlehem, Bethlehem,
      Bethlehem,
Here we go up to Bethlehem
On a cold and frosty morning.

2 We've got to be counted in Bethlehem,
      Bethlehem, Bethlehem,
We've got to be counted in Bethlehem
On a cold and frosty morning.

3 Where shall we stay in Bethlehem,
      Bethlehem, Bethlehem,
Where shall we stay in Bethlehem
On a cold and frosty morning?

Sydney Carter (1915–)

38 MARY HAD A BABY

1 Mary had a baby,
  Yes, Lord,
  Mary had a baby,
  Yes, my Lord,
  Mary had a baby,
  Yes, Lord,
  The people came to Bethlehem
  To see her Son.

2 What did she name him?
  Yes, Lord,
  What did she name him?
  Yes, my Lord,
  What did she name him?
  CHORUS

3 She named him Jesus,
  Yes, Lord,
  She named him Jesus,
  Yes, my Lord,
  She named him Jesus,
  CHORUS

4 Where was he born?
  Yes, Lord,
  Where was he born?
  Yes, my Lord,
  Where was he born?
  CHORUS

5 Born in a stable,
  Yes, Lord,
  Born in a stable,
  Yes, my Lord,
  Born in a stable,
  CHORUS

6 Where did she lay him?
  Yes, Lord,
  Where did she lay him?
  Yes, my Lord,
  Where did she lay him?
  CHORUS

7 Laid him in a manger,
  Yes, Lord,
  Laid him in a manger,
  Yes, my Lord,
  Laid him in a manger,
  CHORUS

Adapted from traditional words by
David Evans (1942–)

39 FOR A GIFT SERVICE

1 When the frost turns the berries red
  Just before Christmas time,
  When the robin wears breast of red
  In the cold mid winter time,
  Then I jump up and down with joy
  And I shout Hip! Hip! Hooray!
  And I thank Lord Jesus Christ who came
  To the earth on Christmas Day.

2 When the time comes to share the toys
  From the Christmas tree tall,
  When the Star shines on girls and boys
  Heaven's here for one and all,
  Then I jump up and down with joy
  And I shout Hip! Hip! Hooray!
  And I thank Lord Jesus Christ who came
  To the earth on Christmas Day.

3 When we bring our gifts to God
  We will gladden his heart,
  When we call other folks to God
  We shall never be apart.
  And we'll jump up and down with joy
  And we'll shout Hip! Hip! Hooray!
  And we'll thank Lord Jesus Christ who
    came
  To the earth on Christmas Day.

Brian Milsom (1926–)

40 THE WORD IS BORN

1 The Word is born this very night:
  Hail, Mary, full of grace!
  A hanging lantern sheds its light
  On Joseph's anxious face.

2 The Word must come in human form,
  In God's redemptive plan.
  A Babe takes every heart by storm,
  But who will heed the Man?

3 The Word is born this very night,
  And humble is the place;
  The world is dark, but hope is bright,
  As sinners look for grace.

4 The Word has come to end the war
  Which Adam first began.
  O bless the Babe who sleeps on straw,
  And listen to the Man!

Fred Pratt Green (1903–)

41 GOD'S GIFT

1 Jesus is God's gift to us,
 Born on Christmas Day.
 How we love to think of him
 Sleeping in the hay!
 The calf said MOO!
 And the lamb said BAA!
 And the donkey stamped its feet;
 And Joseph said HUSH!
 And Mary smiled,
 As kings and shepherds hurried to greet
 The Christ Child!

2 This is why on Christmas Day
 Gifts are on the tree;
 This is why I love to give,
 And others give to me.
 CHORUS

3 Jesus is God's gift to us,
 This and every day.
 How we love to think of him
 Sleeping in the hay!
 CHORUS

The children may say MOO! and BAA! and
stamp their feet

Fred Pratt Green (1903–)

42 FOR A TOY SERVICE

1 We haven't come from far,
 Like wise men did of old;
 We can't bring Jesus myrrh,
 Or frankincense, or gold:
 But here's a bouncing ball,
 And here's a box of bricks,
 And here's a woolly toy:
 So every child can enjoy
 Christmas!

2 We've come from very near,
 Like shepherds did of old;
 But we haven't got a fleece
 For Jesus, if he's cold:
 CHORUS

Fred Pratt Green (1903–)

43 SING HIGH WITH THE HOLLY

1 Sing high with the holly
 And low with the berry;
 All will be gathered

Around my green tree.
 Where have they hidden you
 Child of the manger,
 Child of my childhood
 And seal of my soul?
 They have carved me in stone
 O Child of my passion,
 Bound me in dogma
 And trammelled my will.

2 They have wrapped me in tinsel
 And sold me at counters
 Tuning my song
 To the ring of their till.
 Where can I find you
 O Child of the manger,
 Child of my childhood
 And seal of my soul?
 You can find me as ever
 With blind and with beggar,
 The lame and the prisoner,
 And broken in heart.

3 But finding's not keeping,
 And keeping's not following;
 Follow me home
 To the end of the road.
 Where can I find you
 O Child of the manger,
 Child of my childhood
 And seal of my soul?
 At home with the homeless
 I dine with the outcast
 And if you receive them
 Then there shall I be.

4 Sing high with the holly
 And low with the berry;
 All will be gathered
 Around my green tree.

A.J. Lewis

44 A MESSAGE OF HOPE

1 How dark was the night of his coming!
 How bleak was the wind on the hill!
 How many, who slept till cock-crowing,
 Had little to wake for but ill.
 Good shepherds, who stare into heaven,
 What see you so fair and so rare?
 What glory transfigures your faces?
 What songs are enchanting the air?

2 Those dutiful shepherds saw angels
  Where most of us only see night;
  Their beautiful vision escapes us
  Who cease to believe in the light.
  The song is tossed back into darkness
  By winds that are bitter with hate;
  But shepherds have found in a manger
  That Saviour the ages await.

3 You angels, we see you, we hear you!
  We stand with our backs to the wind!
  The longer we listen, the stronger
  Your message of hope for mankind.
  You sceptics and cynics, forgive us
  For leaving you out in the cold:
  We'll come back with songs of salvation,
  Good news that shall never grow old.

Fred Pratt Green (1903–)

45 GO, TELL THE GOOD NEWS

Go tell it on the mountain,
Over the hills and everywhere:
Go tell it on the mountain,
That Jesus Christ is born.

1 As Mary used to feed him, in her arms he
      gently lay,
  He learned to walk and talk, and together
      they would play.
  CHORUS

2 He worked with his father, Joseph, with
      hammer, nails amd wood
  To make the chairs and tables, and to sell
      them if he could.
  CHORUS

3 He talked to crowds of people, and
      showed them how to live,
  To help the sick and lonely. 'Unto them',
      he said, 'we give'.
  CHORUS

Traditional adapted John Tearnan (1937–)

46 CAROL OF THE UNIVERSE

1 Every star shall sing a carol;
  Every creature, high or low,
  Come and praise the King of Heaven
  By whatever name you know.
  God above, Man below,
  Holy is the name I know.

2 When the King of all creation
  Had a cradle on the earth,
  Holy was the human body,
  Holy was the human birth.
  CHORUS

3 Who can tell what other cradle
  High above the Milky Way
  Still may rock the King of Heaven
  On another Christmas Day?
  CHORUS

4 Who can count how many crosses,
  Still to come or long ago,
  Crucify the King of Heaven?
  Holy is the name I know.
  CHORUS

5 Who can tell what other body
  He will hallow for his own?
  I will praise the Son of Mary,
  Brother of my blood and bone.
  CHORUS

6 Every star and every planet,
  Every creature high and low,
  Come and praise the King of Heaven
  By whatever name you know.
  CHORUS

Sydney Carter (1915–)

47 GOD NEEDS ALL OF US

1 When God Almighty came to be one of us,
  Masking the glory of his golden train,
  Dozens of plain things kindled by accident,
  And they will never be the same again.
  Sing all you midwives, dance all the
      carpenters,
  Sing all the publicans and shepherds too,
  God in his mercy uses the commonplace,
  God on his birthday had a need of you.

2 Splendour of Rome and Local Authority,
  Working on policy with furrowed head,
  Joined to locate Messiah's nativity,
  Just where the prophets had already said.
  Sing all you tax-men, dance the
      Commissioners,
  Sing civil servants and policemen too,
  God in his purpose uses the governments,
  God on his birthday had a need of you.

3 Wise men, they called them, earnest
    astrologers,
  Watching for meaning in the moving stars,
  Science or fancy, learned or laughable,
  Theirs was a vision that was brought to
    pass.
  Sing all you wise men, dance all the
    scientists,
  Whether your theories are false or true,
  God uses knowledge, God uses ignorance,
  God on his birthday had a need of you.

4 Sing, all creation, made for his purposes,
  Called by his providence to live and move:
  None is unwanted, none insignificant,
  Love needs a universe of folk to love.
  Old men and maidens, young men and
    children,
  Black ones and coloured ones and white
    ones too,
  God on his birthday, and to eternity,
  God took upon himself the need of you.

Michael Hewlett (1916–)

48 MARY'S CHILD

1 Born in the night,
  Mary's Child,
  A long way from your home;
  Coming in need,
  Mary's Child,
  Born in a borrowed room.

2 Clear shining light,
  Mary's Child,
  Your face lights up our way;
  Light of the world,
  Mary's Child,
  Dawn on our darkened day.

3 Truth of our life,
  Mary's Child,
  You tell us God is good;
  Prove it is true,
  Mary's Child,
  Go to your cross of wood.

4 Hope of the world,
  Mary's Child,
  You're coming soon to reign;
  King of the earth,
  Mary's Child,
  Walk in our streets again.

Geoffrey Ainger (1925–)

49 JESUS NEEDS US

1 You needed a stable the night you were
    born,
  A manger to serve as your bed,
  You needed a girl from a country town
  And a light where the cattle fed;
  Then as you grew
  In wisdom and strength
  And came to know your God
  You needed a joiner's workshop
  Beside a village road.

2 You needed a school boy to give you his
    lunch,
  A little to feed a great crowd,
  You needed the fish and the home-made
    bread
  And you asked for the help of God;
  As you drew near
  To passion and death
  And thought of trial and cross
  You needed a street-girl's ointment
  To signify your loss.

3 You needed a donkey to ride into town,
  A friend's room for supper that night,
  You needed a band of common men
  And their songs in the evening light;
  Out in the dark
  While kneeling in prayer
  In grim Gethsemane
  You needed to have watch with you
  Your friends from Galilee.

4 You needed a stranger to help with your
    cross,
  A Simon to carry your load,
  You needed his back in the jeers and shouts
  And the whips on the narrow road;
  But for his strength
  You wouldn't have been
  Hoisted up on high
  And we wouldn't have seen your glory
  Under the lowering sky.

Geoffrey Ainger (1925–)

50 AMEN! AMEN!

Amen,
Amen,
Amen,
Amen.

1 See the little baby,
  Lying in a manger,
  One cold Christmas morning;

2 See him in the temple,
  Talking to the elders,
  Amazed at his wisdom;

3 See him at the seaside,
  Preaching there and healing
  The blind and the feeble;

4 Yes he is my Saviour,
  Jesus died to save us,
  And rose up at Easter;

5 All say Hallelujah,
  Sing through his Kingdom
  The Lord is my Saviour.

Negro spiritual adapted Peter D. Smith (1938–)

51 THE MAN JESUS

1 In that land which we call holy,
  From of old a land of strife,
  Lived a Man whose birth was lowly:
  Great our debt to that one life.

2 Where the Roman legions sweated,
  In a world where might was right,
  Lived a Man whose love defeated
  Deadlier foes than soldiers fight.

3 Where a proud and subject nation
  Learned to scorn each lesser breed,
  Lived a Man whose true compassion
  Knew no bounds of race or creed.

4 Where men studied to be righteous,
  Strict to keep each trivial ban,
  Lived a Man who came to teach us
  Love of God is love of man.

5 Where God's People long expected
  God would reign, or God had lied,
  Lived a Man they all rejected,
  Lived the God they crucified.

6 This our faith: he lives for ever!
  Love redeems, though it is slain!
  This his Church's whole endeavour:
  So to live that Christ may reign.

Fred Pratt Green (1903–)

52 JESUS TEMPTED - 1

1 Savagely beat the desert sun,
  Jesus, upon your brow;
  You had to face the fiercest tests
  That anyone could know.

2 When you were in the wilderness,
  There by the Spirit led,
  Jesus, you could have used your power
  To turn the stones to bread.

3 You could have leapt from Temple-top
  To win the crowd's applause,
  By such a swift and simple way
  Advance the Kingdom's cause.

4 Jesus, you could have gained the world
  And used an emperor's might
  To end injustice everywhere:
  But would that way be right?

5 When we are faced with several ways,
  And wonder which is best:
  Guide us to know what you would do
  And then reject the rest.

Cyril G. Hambly (1931–)

53 JESUS TEMPTED - 2

1 When he was baptized in Jordan
  Jesus knew his chosen role:
  Ready now for time of testing
  In the desert of the soul.

2 Starved of bread to feed the body,
  Starved of rest to feed the brain,
  Starved of friends to feed the spirit,
  Jesus daily bore the strain.

3 During six long weeks of trial,
  Evil masquerades as good:
  Points false roads to instant lordship,
  Tempts him with the Word of God.

4 He attacks the great imposter:
  Evil shall not win this day!
  Ready now to serve his calling,
  Sets his face Jerusalem way.

5 When our turn comes to be tempted,
  As we meet each vital choice,
  Make us wise and make us willing,
  Lord of life, to heed your voice.

Bernard Braley (1924–)

54 THE MAN ON THE BED

1 When the friends of a man
Who was crippled and ill
Decided to bring him
To Jesus to heal,
To prove their concern,
Though it needs no proof,
When they couldn't get near him
They took off the roof.

2 Well, the sight was enough
To make anyone stare —
A man on a bed
Coming down through the air!
But Jesus, perceiving
The work they had done,
Said his sins were forgiven,
His illness all gone.

3 So I know, when I do things
For anyone's sake,
What matters to God is
The trouble I take.
And if it's my friend,
Like the man on the bed,
He'll accept what I do
And reward him instead.

Michael Hewlett (1916–)

55 HEAL US, LORD JESUS

1 When Jesus the healer walked through
    Galilee,
Heal us, heal us today:
The deaf came to hear and the blind came
    to see,
Heal us, Lord Jesus.

2 A poor paralytic was let through the roof,
Heal us, heal us today:
His sins were forgiven, he walked as a
    proof,
Heal us, Lord Jesus.

3 The death of his daughter caused Jairus to
    weep,
Heal us, heal us today:
The Lord took her hand and then raised
    her from sleep,
Heal us, Lord Jesus.

4 A deaf and dumb spirit had made a boy mad
Heal us, heal us today:
His father had faith — Jesus healed the
    young lad,
Heal us, Lord Jesus.

5 When blind Bartimaeus cried out to the
    Lord,
Heal us, heal us today:
His faith made him whole and his sight was
    restored,
Heal us, Lord Jesus.

6 He sent the twelve out to the country in
    twos,
Heal us, heal us today:
To heal all the sick and to spread the good
    news,
Heal us, Lord Jesus.

7 The lepers are healed and the demons cast
    out,
Heal us, heal us today:
The lame leap for joy and the dumb laugh
    and shout,
Heal us, Lord Jesus.

8 We've just as much sickness and suffering
    today,
Heal us, heal us today:
So gather together for healing to pray,
Heal us, Lord Jesus.

Peter D. Smith (1938–)

56 THEY LEFT THEIR NETS

1 Two men were fishing the Sea of Galilee,
Two men were fishing the Sea of Galilee;
Jesus he came along and said, 'Come
    follow me',
And they left their nets to follow him,
And they left their nets to follow him.

2 Mending their nets were two brothers in a
    boat,
Mending their nets were two brothers in a
    boat;
Jesus he called to them and said, 'It's time
    to go',
And they left their nets to follow him,
And they left their nets to follow him.

3 James, John and Peter with Andrew
    worked each day,

James, John and Peter with Andrew
  worked each day;
Jesus he spoke to them and said, 'I am the
  Way',
And they left their nets to follow him,
And they left their nets to follow him.

John Tearnan (1937–)

57 FOLLOW ME!

1 Fisherman Peter, on the sea,
Drop your net, boy, and follow me!
Fisherman Peter, on the sea,
Drop you net, boy, and follow me!

2 Rich young ruler, plain to see,
Can't love money and follow me!
Rich young ruler, plain to see,
Can't love money and follow me!

3 Lonely Zacchaeus in the tree,
Love your neighbour and follow me!
Lonely Zacchaeus in the tree,
Love your neighbour and follow me!

4 Nicodemus Pharisee,
New life comes when you follow me!
Nicodemus Pharisee,
New life comes when you follow me!

5 Doubting Thomas, come and see,
Stop your doubting and follow me!
Doubting Thomas, come and see,
Stop your doubting and follow me!

Traditional

58 THE LIVING BREAD

1 I saw the Man from Galilee
Who told a message new.
The hungry crowd had gathered round
To see what he could do.
And in his words was hope;
And in his hands was bread.
'Come share this bread
And share my life –
My life for you,' he said.

2 I saw a boy with barley loaves;
He had some small fish too.
'I can't do much, but I can share:
Lord Jesus, it's for you.

For in your words is hope
And in you hands is bread.
I'll share my bread
And know your love –
Your life for me,' he said.

3 I saw a rich young man, who came
To speak to Jesus too.
'I want to live, I don't know how,'
He said, 'What can I do?'
And Jesus answered, 'This
Is life, to share your bread.
Sell all you have,
Give to the poor,
Life can be yours,' he said.

4 I saw the whole world in the eyes
Of one small hungry boy.
There is no hope, there is no life,
There is no sign of joy.
And how can there be hope,
Where people have no bread?
They struggle on
And try to live,
But life hangs by a thread:

5 Yet Jesus shows us hope,
For in his hands is bread;
Bread for the world
If all will share –
He is the living Bread.

George Chalmers (1937–)

59 JESUS LORD OF GLORY

1 Jesus is the Lord of Glory:
  Reign in me, Lord Jesus!
Jesus is the Light of the World:
  Shine in me, Lord Jesus!
Jesus is the Friend of sinners:
  Set me free, Lord Jesus!
Jesus is the Way:
  May I walk in it!
Jesus is the Truth:
  May I believe in it!
Jesus is the Life:
  May I share in it!
Way and Truth and Life.

Fred Pratt Green (1903–)

60 THE LORD'S DAY

1 This is the day,
This is the day that the Lord has made,
That the Lord has made,
We will rejoice,
We will rejoice and be glad in it,
And be glad in it.
This is the day that the Lord has made,
We will rejoice and be glad in it.
This is the day that the Lord has made.

2 This is the day,
This is the day when he rose again,
When he rose again,
We will rejoice,
We will rejoice and be glad in it,
And be glad in it.
This is the day when he rose again,
We will rejoice and be glad in it.
This is the day when he rose again.

3 This is the day,
This is the day when the Spirit came,
When the spirit came.
We will rejoice,
We will rejoice and be glad in it,
And be glad in it.
This is the day when the Spirit came,
We will rejoice and be glad in it.
This is the day when the Spirit came.

Traditional

61 THE LORD'S PRAYER

1 Our Father who art in heaven,
Hallowed be thy Name,
Thy Kingdom come, thy will be done,
Hallowed be thy Name,

2 On earth as it is in heaven,
Hallowed be thy Name,
Give us this day our daily bread,
Hallowed be thy Name.

3 Forgive us all our trespasses,
Hallowed be thy Name,
As we forgive those who trespass against
us,
Hallowed be thy Name.

4 And lead us not into temptation,
Hallowed be thy Name,
But deliver us from all that is evil,
Hallowed be thy Name

5 For thine is the Kingdom, the Power and
the Glory,
Hallowed be thy Name,
For ever and for ever and ever,
Hallowed be thy Name.

6 Amen, Amen, it shall be so,
Hallowed be thy Name,
Amen, Amen, it shall be so,
Hallowed be thy Name.

Holy Scripture

62 ON THE JERICHO ROAD

1 A man had been robbed of all he had
On the Jericho Road;
They beat him up and left him for dead.
'It happens like that,' the Master said,
'On the Jericho Road.'

2 A Priest and a Levite passed him by
On the Jericho Road;
They taught the Law but they didn't try
To help the man who was left to die
On the Jericho Road.

3 By chance a Samaritan passed that way
On the Jericho Road;
In spite of the worst the Jews could say,
He did his best for the man who lay
On the Jericho Road.

4 He bandaged him up with loving skill
On the Jericho Road,
And found an inn to care for him till
He came again (and settled the bill)
On the Jericho Road.

5 'To be a neighbour,' the Master said,
'On the Jericho Road,
Is to show compassion as that man did.'
For even faith without deeds is dead
On the Jericho Road,
On the Jericho Road,
On the Jericho Road.

Fred Pratt Green (1903–)

63 THE LOST IS FOUND

1 Where, oh where's my silver piece?
Where, oh where? Where, oh where?
Where, oh where's my silver piece?
Where, oh where's it gone?
Searching high and searching low,
Searching high, searching low;
Oh, what joy when it is found!
Joy when it is found!
Let's join hands and dance for joy,
Stamp for joy, clap for joy;
Let's join hands and dance for joy,
Stamp and clap for joy!

2 Where, oh where's my little lamb?
Where, oh where? Where, oh where?
Where, oh where's my little lamb?
Where, oh where's he gone?
Searching here and searching there,
Searching here, searching there;
Oh, what joy when he is found,
Joy when he is found!
CHORUS

3 Where, oh where's my wand'ring son?
Where, oh where? Where, oh where?
Where, oh where's my wand'ring son?
Where, oh where's he gone?
Looking far and looking long,
Looking far, looking long;
Oh, what joy when he comes home,
Joy when he comes home!
CHORUS

Cecily Taylor (1930–)

64 THE PRODIGAL COMES HOME

1 He came from a far-away land
And he knew not that love was at hand.
He looked none in the face,
He felt only disgrace,
For he saw not forgiveness, but shame.
Put a ring on his hand and
Shoes on his feet,
Put a ring on his hand and
Shoes on his feet,
Let's be merry and dance and
Make him a feast,
Let's be merry and make him a feast.

2 He arrives within sight of his home,
There's rapturous welcome to come,
Someone's meeting him now,
Someone's greeting him now,
And he knows he's no longer alone.
CHORUS

3 The agonised days are all done,
Life returns to the prodigal son.
Taken back to the fold
He finds blessings untold
Where creation is gathered in one.
CHORUS

Chris Rogers (1922–) from the Swedish by
Anders Frostenson (1906–)

65 JESUS THE LORD

1 Jesus the Lord said: 'I am the Bread,
The Bread of Life for mankind am I,
The Bread of Life for mankind am I,
The Bread of Life for mankind am I.'
Jesus the Lord said: 'I am the Bread,
The Bread of Life for mankind am I.'

2 Jesus the Lord said: 'I am the Way,
The true and living Way am I,
The true and living Way am I,
The true and living Way am I.'
Jesus the Lord said: 'I am the Way,
The true and living Way am I.'

3 Jesus the Lord said: 'I am the Light,
The one true Light of the world am I,
The one true Light of the world am I,
The one true Light of the world am I.'
Jesus the Lord said: 'I am the Light,
The one true Light of the world am I.'

4 Jesus the Lord said: 'I am the Shepherd,
The one good Shepherd of the sheep am I,
The one good Shepherd of the sheep am I,
The one good Shepherd of the sheep am I.'
Jesus the Lord said: 'I am the Shepherd,
The one good Shepherd of the sheep am I.'

5 Jesus the Lord said: 'I am the Life,
The Resurrection and the Life am I,
The Resurrection and the Life am I,
The Resurrection and the Life am I.'
Jesus the Lord said: 'I am the Life,
The Resurrection and the Life am I.'

Translated from the Urdu by
Dermott Monihan (1906-1957)

66 JUDAS AND MARY

1 Said Judas to Mary, 'Now what will you
    do
  With your ointment so rich and so rare?
  'I'll pour it all over the feet of the Lord
  And I'll wipe it away with my hair,' she
    said,
  'I'll wipe it away with my hair.'

2 'Oh Mary, oh Mary, oh think of the poor
  This ointment it could have been sold;
  And think of the blankets and think of
    the bread
  You could buy with the silver and gold,'
    he said,
  'You could buy with the silver and gold.'

3 'Tomorrow, tomorrow I'll think of the poor,
  Tomorrow,' she said, 'not today;
  For dearer than all of the poor of the world
  Is my love who is going away,' she said,
  'My love who is going away.'

4 Said Jesus to Mary, 'Your love is so deep,
  Today you may do as you will;
  Tomorrow, you say, I am going away,
  But my body I leave with you still,' he
    said,
  'My body I leave with you still.'

5 'The poor of the world are my body,' he
    said,
  'To the end of the world they shall be;
  The bread and the blankets you give to
    the poor
  You'll find you have given to me,' he said,
  'You'll find you have given to me.'

6 'My body will hang on the cross of the
    world
  Tomorrow,' he said, 'and today,
  And Martha and Mary will find me again
  And wash all my sorrow away,' he said,
  'And wash all my sorrow away.'

Sydney Carter (1915–)

67 SHEEP AND GOATS

The chorus is sung twice each time
1 When the nations meet before him,
  And the King in judgement sits,
  To the right and left he'll send them,
  This way 'sheep' and that way 'goats'.

'When you cared,' he shall say,
'You were helping me that day.'

2 'Lord, whenever did we see you?
  When were you without a meal?
  When were you thrown into prison,
  Dressed in rags or deathly pale?'
  'When you cared,' he shall say,
  'You were helping me that day.'

3 'Lord, whenever did we see you
  Thirsty on a dusty road?
  When were you in need of shelter
  And the comfort of a bed?'
  'When we passed,' he shall say,
  'You saw me and turned away.'

4 To the 'sheep' the King will beckon:
  'Sit now at my Father's hand —
  Enter and possess the Kingdom,
  Ready since the world was planned.'
  'When you cared,' he shall say,
  'You were helping me that day.'

David Mowbray (1938–)

68 PALM SUNDAY - 1

1 Look, a strange procession moves
  On the hill of Olivet;
  Headed by that humble one —
  On a patient donkey set,
  Circled by the friends he loves.

2 Look, our Lord is riding there —
  Carried by that quiet beast,
  Coming to Jerusalem
  Ready for the sacred feast!
  Crowds are jostling everywhere.

3 Look, the people take from trees
  Palms to put before his feet.
  Fronds are waved upon the air;
  Questions asked in every street —
  Easy now, the crowds to please!

4 Look, the faithful beam with pride,
  Shrill hosannas break the air,
  Never was a day like this!
  Faces seem without a care
  For this radiant, royal ride.

5 Look, today his friends are here,
  Met his kingship to acclaim:
  Our hosannas, we will shout,
  Love, in every age the same,
  Holds us true, and keeps you near!

Cyril G. Hambly (1931–)

69 PALM SUNDAY - 2

1 Trotting, trotting through Jerusalem,
  Jesus, sitting on a donkey's back,
  Children waving branches, singing,
  'Happy is he that comes in the name of the
    Lord!

2 Many people in Jerusalem
  Thought he should have come on a mighty
    horse
  Leading all the Jews to battle –
  'Happy is he that comes in the name of the
    Lord!'

3 Many people in Jerusalem
  Were amazed to see such a quiet man
  Trotting, trotting on a donkey –
  'Happy is he that comes in the name of the
    Lord!'

4 Trotting, trotting through Jerusalem,
  Jesus, sitting on a donkey's back,
  Let us join the children singing,
  'Happy is he that comes in the name of the
    Lord!'

Eric Reid (1936–1970)

70 THREE CHEERS FOR JESUS CHRIST

1 The crowds fill the streets as they welcome
    their King,
  And they cut down palm branches to wave
    as they sing.
  His friends bring a donkey on which he
    can ride
  While the children are walking so close by
    his side.
  'Hosanna! Hosanna! Hosanna!' they sing,
  'Hosanna! Hosanna!' to Jesus their King;
  'Three cheers and Hooray!' is how we would
    say,
  'Hosanna.'

2 He goes to the Temple and there he is sad
  When he sees all the merchants whose
    ways are so bad.
  They cheat and they lie while they're
    selling their wares,
  So Christ tells them the Temple's the place
    for men's prayers.
  CHORUS

3 He meets his disciples for something to eat,
  Then he gets up from supper and washes
    their feet.
  They look on in wonder at this act of love,
  But he's shown that a King is the one who
    will serve.
  CHORUS

Barry Miller (1942–)

71 A HYMN FOR HOLY WEEK
Selected verses may be chosen

1 All is ready for the Feast!
  Every Jew is wondering how
  God will liberate them now.

2 Pilate, fearful of revolt
  He, at all costs, must avert,
  Puts the Legion on alert.

3 Listen! Galilean crowds
  Hail the Man from Nazareth,
  Jesus, riding to his death.

4 What authority he wields!
  With a whip of cords he clears
  Temple courts of profiteers!

5 Watched by priests and pharisees,
  All he says and all he does
  Fans the hatred of his foes.

6 Now he gathers those he loves
  In a room where bread and wine
  Turn to sacrament and sign.

7 In that dark betrayal night,
  Moved by hope, or fear or greed,
  Judas sets about his deed.

8 Jesus in the olive grove,
  Waiting for a traitor's kiss,
  Rises free from bitterness.

9 As he wakes his comrades up,
  Torches flicker in the glen:
  Shadows turn to marching men.

10 In that dawn of blows and lies
   Church and State conspire to kill,
   Hang three rebels on a hill.

11 Innocent and guilty drown
   In a flood of blood and sweat,
   How much darker can it get?

12 How much darker must it be
   For a God to see and care
   That men perish in despair?

13 It is God himself who dies!
   God in man shall set us free:
   God as man — and only he.

14 Let him claim us as his own,
   We will serve as best we can
   Such a God and such a Man!

   *Additional verse (written for proper
   conclusion when limited number of
   verses are sung):*

15 What does our salvation cost?
   Jesus, we shall never know
   All you gave and all we owe.

Fred Pratt Green (1903–)

72 ROMAN SOLDIERS MARCHING

1 Dark against an eastern sky,
   Roman soldiers marching;
   No one cheered as they went by,
   Roman soldiers marching.
   Disciplined to beat their foe,
   Roman soldiers marching:
   As a boy he watched them go,
   Jesus watched them marching.

2 Jewish boy beside the Way
   Watched the soldiers marching;
   They will come another day,
   Roman soldiers marching.
   Then with orders to fulfil,
   Roman soldiers marching,
   They will hang him on a hill,
   Roman soldiers watching.

3 He who dies is Lord of all,
   He shall reign for ever;
   Empires rise and empires fall,
   He shall reign for ever.

When he comes, our Prince of Peace,
He shall reign for ever;
All oppression then shall cease,
He shall reign for ever!

Fred Pratt Green (1903–)

73 WHO IS HE?

1 Who was the other who died on the hill?
   Who was the other closed in for the kill?
   One was a robber and one was a thief —
   But who was the third man whose life was
     so brief?
   Who do men say that I am?
   Who do men say that I am?

2 Some say a prophet come back from the
     dead,
   Some an idealist but rather misled;
   Some say a teacher or King of the Jews,
   And some say God's son who had no
     power to choose.
   Who do men say that I am?
   Who do men say that I am?

3 Some say a leader upholding the right,
   Some say a rebel with no guts to fight.
   Some say a legend, and some say a fool,
   And some — an impostor playing it
     cool.
   Who do men say that I am?
   Who do men say that I am?

4 Who was the other who died on the hill?
   Who was the other closed in for the kill?
   One was a robber and one was a thief —
   But who was the third man whose life was
     so brief?
   Who do you say that I am?
   Who do you say that I am?

Cecily Taylor (1930–)

*The Editors feel the colloquial usage of 'guts'
in verse 3 is entirely appropriate in its context*

74 WERE YOU THERE?

1 Were you there when they crucifed my
     Lord?
   Were you there when they crucified my
     Lord?
   Oh — sometimes it causes me to tremble,
     tremble, tremble;
   Were you there when they crucified my
     Lord?

2 Were you there when they nailed him
   to the tree?
Were you there when they nailed him
   to the tree?
Oh — sometimes it causes me to tremble,
   tremble, tremble;
Were you there when they nailed him
   to the tree?

3 Were you there when they pierced him in
   the side?
Were you there when they pierced him in
   the side?
Oh — sometimes it causes me to tremble,
   tremble, tremble;
Were you there when they pierced him in
   the side?

4 Were you there when the sun refused to
   shine?
Were you there when the sun refused to
   shine?
Oh — sometimes it causes me to tremble,
   tremble, tremble;
Were you there when the sun refused to
   shine?

5 Were you there when they laid him in the
   tomb?
Were you there when they laid him in the
   tomb?
Oh — sometimes it causes me to tremble,
   tremble, tremble;
Were you there when they laid him in the
   tomb?

6 Were you there when he rose from out the
   tomb?
Were you there when he rose from out the
   tomb?
Oh — sometimes it causes me to tremble,
   tremble, tremble;
Were you there when he rose from out the
   tomb?

Negro spiritual adapted Peter D. Smith
(1938–)

75 PASSION CAROL

1 God made the tree that gave the wood;
   Sorrowing tree, that ever should
   Be made to form a Cross,
   Be made to form a Cross.

2 God made the man that felled that tree;
   Sorrowing man, that ever he
   Should help to make a Cross,
   Should help to make a Cross.

3 God made the one who drove the nails;
   Sorrowing one: all history rails
   On him, who raised that Cross,
   On him, who raised that Cross.

4 God made us too, who cause his pain;
   Sorrowing links in the human chain
   Of all who make his Cross,
   Of all who make his Cross.

5 God was tnat man, who once was killed;
   Sorrowing Lord, whose mercy willed
   In love, to bear that Cross,
   In love, to bear that Cross.

Cyril G. Hambly (1931–)

76 THE TRIUMPH OF THE CROSS

1 Sing, all Christians, of the triumph
   On a rough-hewn cross of wood
   Where the Christ, courageous sufferer,
   Conquers evil through his good;
   This the method God has chosen
   To redeem our human kind,
   Change the folly of our choices
   To the wisdom of God's mind.

2 Sing, all Christians, of the God who
   Since the dawn of earthly time
   Knew in Christ the total burden
   Of a world possessed by crime.
   Sing, all Christians, of the coming
   Timely made by Christ to earth,
   Living as a suffering servant,
   Bringing his new age to birth.

3 By his living thus in history,
   By his dying on the tree,
   By his suffering mind and body,
   Once for all, for you and me,
   By the travail of his spirit
   Plunging deep to dark despair,
   Through such costly Godlike action
   For the race locked in his care:

4 Thus, all Christians, this Messiah,
Risen now from conquered death,
Gains for us our God's forgiveness,
Takes all fear from dying breath.
Present with us in the future
Lives our suffering, serving Friend.
Sing, all Christians, of this Mystery,
Christ in glory without end.

Bernard Braley (1924–)

77 CHRIST?

1 See him quietly standing there,
A child without a home,
No food, no bed, no friends to share,
Just lost and left alone.

2 See him quietly crying there,
Body just skin and bone,
No food, no bed, no friends to share,
Just lost and left alone.

3 See him quietly sleeping there
On a step of stone,
No food, no bed, no friends to share,
Just lost and left alone.

4 Leave him quietly dying there,
A child without a home,
No food, no bed, no friends to share –
Christ, lost and left alone?

John Tearnan (1937–)

78 DEATH AND RESURRECTION

1 Jesus in the garden,
Sad and left alone,
Soldiers come to take him;
His friends have run for home.

2 Jesus in the courtroom,
Sad and left alone,
People come to mock him
In robe and crown of thorns.

3 Jesus on the hillside,
Sad and left alone,
In the silent darkness
He dies there on his own.

4 Hiding in their home,
Disciples lock the door,
Frightened of the people;
They go outside no more.

5 Disciples in the room
Feel sadness turn to joy,
Know there's work for them to do,
Throw open wide the door.

6 Disciples meet the crowds
To share their joy with them,
Dance and sing to tell about
The man from Nazareth.

John Tearnan (1937–)

79 THINGS WE CAN'T EXPLAIN

1 The cat hunts the bird and the lion the
deer;
The rose has its thorn, and the heart has its
fear;
We cannot say why – yet the Father is
near.

2 While Mary was rocking her baby asleep,
The orders of Herod made other eyes
weep;
We cannot say why – yet God's wisdom is
deep.

3 When life's like a raft that the stormy
winds toss,
When shaken by sorrow or battered by
loss,
He calls us to share all he won on the
cross.

4 The rose has its thorn, and the heart has its
fear;
The night may seem dark, but the dawn
will appear;
In time we shall know that the Father is
near.

Basil E. Bridge (1927–)

80 AT EASTERTIDE

1 When Easter to the dark world came,
Fair flowers glowed like scarlet flame:
At Eastertide, at Eastertide,
O glad was the world at Eastertide.

2 When Mary in the garden walked,
And with her risen Master talked:
CHORUS

3 When John and Peter in their gloom
Met angels at the empty tomb:
CHORUS

4 When Thomas' heart with grief was black,
Then Jesus like a King came back:
CHORUS

5 And friend to friend in wonder said:
'The Lord is risen from the dead!'
CHORUS

6 This Eastertide with joyful voice
We'll sing 'The Lord is King! rejoice!'
CHORUS

W.H. Hamilton (1886 - 1952)

81 LOVE IS COME AGAIN

1 Now the green blade riseth from the
buried grain,
Wheat that in the dark earth many days
has lain.
Love lives again, that with the dead has
been;
Love is come again, like wheat that
springeth green.

2 In the grave they laid him, Love whom
men had slain,
Thinking that never he would wake again;
Laid in the earth like grain that sleeps
unseen,
Love is come again, like wheat that
springeth green.

3 Forth he came at Easter, like the risen
grain,
He that for three days in the grave had
lain.
Quick from the dead my risen Lord is seen;
Love is come again, like wheat that
springeth green.

4 When our hearts are wintry, grieving, or in
pain,
Thy touch can call us back to life again.
Fields of our hearts that dead and bare
have been;
Love is come again, like wheat that
springeth green.

J.M.C. Crum (1872-1958)

82 ROLL ON, EASTER

1 Winter rolls past,
Leaves and flowers open fast,
Easter will come at last,
Hallelujah!

(To be sung as a round: Sing 'Hurrah'
the last time)

*Translated from the French by Emily
Chisholm (1910–)*

83 OUR CHRIST IS RISEN

1 This joyful Eastertide,
What need is there for grieving?
Cast all your care aside
And be not unbelieving:
*Come, share our Easter joy
That death could not imprison,
Nor any power destroy,
Our Christ, who is arisen,
Arisen, arisen, arisen!*

2 No work for him is vain,
No faith in him mistaken,
For Easter makes it plain
His Kingdom is not shaken:
CHORUS

3 Then put your trust in Christ,
In waking or in sleeping.
His grace on earth sufficed;
He'll never quit his keeping:
CHORUS

Fred Pratt Green (1903–)

84 THROUGH HIS RESURRECTION

1 God came in Jesus
Human life sharing:
Gave his life for us,
Suffered and died;
Then, Resurrection!
Death could not hold him;
By love's perfection
Death was defied.

2 Then, as they waited,
All of a sudden,
Strong and elated,
Freed of all cares;
With no misgiving,
Joyful apostles
Knew that his living
Spirit was theirs.

3 So let us greet his
Coming among us;
Let us still meet his
Love with delight;
Through resurrection,
Joyfully taking
Love's new direction
Flooded with light.

4 He will be coming,
Mighty and glorious,
Universe humming
Loud in acclaim;
Through resurrection
Of all creation
Brought to perfection,
Praising his name.

Alan Gaunt (1935–)

85 EASTER CAROL

1 After darkness, light;
After Winter, Spring;
After dying, life:
Alleluia!

2 Take his body down;
Lay it in the tomb;
Love has overcome:
Alleluia!

3 Turn away in grief;
Turn away in faith;
Celebrate his death:
Alleluia!

4 Come whatever may
God will have his way;
Welcome, Easter Day:
Alleluia!

Fred Pratt Green (1903–)

86 HE'S BACK!

1 He's back in the land of the living,
The man we decided to kill;
He's standing among us, forgiving
Our guilt of Good-Friday-hill.
He calls us to share in his rising,
To abandon the grave of our past;
He offers us present and future,
A world that is open and vast.

2 He's back in a world where the living
Are robbing each other of joy,
Where men for prestige and destruction
The powers of nature employ.
From lofty respectable motives
Are crosses erected today,
For people put people on trial
And evil is having its way.

3 But crosses are also the symbols
Of love that is given and spent;
The signs of our hope and survival,
Of Easter defeating our Lent.
Through men of compassion, responding
To rise against hunger and hell,
New life will arise from the ashes
Of hatred, all will be well!

Fred Kaan (1929–)

87 CHRIST IS ALIVE!

1 Christ is alive! Let Christians sing.
His cross stands empty to the sky.
Let streets and homes with praises ring.
His love in death shall never die.

2 Christ is alive! No longer bound
To distant years in Palestine
He comes to claim the here and now
And conquer every place and time.

3 Not throned above, remotely high,
Untouched, unmoved by human pains
But daily, in the midst of life,
Our Saviour with the Father reigns.

4 In every insult, rift and war
Where colour, scorn or wealth divide
He suffers still, yet loves the more,
And lives, though ever crucified.

5 Christ is alive! Ascendant Lord,
He rules the world his Father made
Till, in the end, his love adored
Shall be to every man displayed.

Brian A. Wren (1936–)

88 LORD OF THE DANCE

1 I danced in the morning
When the world was begun,
And I danced in the moon
And the stars and the sun;
And I came down from heaven
And I danced on the earth,
At Bethlehem
I had my birth
'Dance then, wherever you may be,
I am the Lord of the Dance,' said he,
'And I'll lead you all wherever you may
*   be,*
And I'll lead you all in the Dance,' said he.

2 I danced for the scribe
And the pharisee,
But they would not dance
And they wouldn't follow me.
I danced for the fishermen,
For James and John —
They came with me
And the dance went on.
CHORUS

3 I danced on the Sabbath
And I cured the lame;
The holy people
Said it was a shame.
They whipped and they stripped
And they hung me on high,
And they left me there
On a cross to die.
CHORUS

4 I danced on a Friday
When the sky turned black;
It's hard to dance
With the devil on your back.
They buried my body
And they thought I'd gone —
But I am the Dance,
And I still go on.
CHORUS

5 They cut me down
And I leapt up high;
'I am the Life
That'll never, never die.
I'll live in you
If you'll live in me;
I am the Lord
Of the Dance,' said he.
CHORUS
Sydney Carter (1915–)

89 PETER SPEAKS

1 One morning on that misty shore
We found a meal prepared,
And ate together one meal more
With him, our risen Lord.

2 Three times he asked me, face to face,
If I were still his man.
It's thanks to his amazing grace,
Yes, I am still his man!

3 And if you, too, deny your Lord,
Although it be but once,
You'll hear the same forgiving word
And have your second chance.

4 For some are called a second time,
And some more times than this;
And only those who follow him
Know what all others miss.

Fred Pratt Green (1903–)

90 RESURRECTION'S REAL

1 Christ naming faithful Mary,
Forgiving Peter's fall,
Christ showing questing Thomas,
Declaring peace to all.
Christ breaking bread at supper,
In blessing of a meal,
So proving to disciples
That Resurrection's real.

2 Christ charging the defeated,
Providing them new power,
Christ sending rock-like Peter
To serve his present hour;
Disciples bound together
In sharing of a meal,
So preaching to the nations
That Resurrection's real.

3 Church certain of the presence
Of Christ the Living One,
Church suffering and serving
For each and every one,
Church breaking bread together
In Mystery of a meal,
The Church of God declaring
That Resurrection's real.

Bernard Braley (1924–)

CHRIST AND

OUR DISCIPLESHIP

**in which we sing of the saving grace
of our Lord and consider what it
means to be his disciple.**

Recommended hymns from standard books

91 SALVATION

1 Salvation! There's no better word
  For what Christ does for me:
  He saves me from repented sins
  And sets my spirit free.
  O save me absolutely, Lord,
  That I may play my part
  As your disciple, daily more
  Mature in mind and heart.

2 Salvation! There's no better word
  For what Christ offers us:
  The love that died for you and me
  Upon a Roman cross.
  As servants of your Kingdom, Lord,
  O never let us rest
  Until your love and justice reach
  The needy and oppressed.

3 Salvation! There's no better word
  For all Christ came to do:
  His peace removes the barricades
  And lets forgiveness through.
  O fill your universal Church
  With wisdom, Lord, and love;
  And save this power-hungry world
  With power from above!

Fred Pratt Green (1903–)

92 LIFE IS GREAT

1 Life is great! So sing about it,
  As we can and as we should —
  Shops and buses, towns and people,
  Village, farmland, field and wood.
  Life is great and life is given,
  Life is lovely, free and good.

2 Life is great! — whatever happens,
  Snow or sunshine, joy or pain,
  Hardship, grief or disillusion,
  Suffering that I can't explain —
  Life is great if someone loves me,
  Holds my hand and calls my name.

3 Love is great! — the love of lovers,
  Whispered words and longing eyes;
  Love that gazes at the cradle
  Where a child of loving lies;
  Love that lasts when youth has faded,
  Bends with age, but never dies.

4 Love is giving and receiving —
   Boy and girl, or friend with friend.
   Love is bearing and forgiving
   All the hurts that hate can send.
   Love's the greatest way of living,
   Hoping, trusting to the end.

5 God is great! In Christ he loved us,
   As we should, but never can —
   Love that suffered, hoped and trusted
   When disciples turned and ran,
   Love that broke through death for ever.
   Praise that loving, living Man!

Brian A. Wren (1936–)

93 NICODEMUS

1 Nicodemus comes by night
   Seeking him who is the Light,
   Fearful if he comes by day
   He will give himself away.

2 Nicodemus must find out
   What salvation is about;
   He, the worthiest of men,
   Must, like us, be born again.

3 Scarcely he believes his ears,
   Rabbi, he, these many years!
   That he does not turn aside
   Proves he overcomes his pride.

4 On a day when cowards run
   He declares whose side he's on;
   Strangest of all gifts, he gives
   Space in death — to One who lives.

Fred Pratt Green (1903–)

94 TAKE UP YOUR CROSS

1 Lord, for the years your love has kept and
      guided,
   Urged and inspired us, cheered us on our
      way,
   Sought us and saved us, pardoned and
      provided,
   Lord of the years, we bring our thanks
      today.

2 Lord, for that Word, the Word of life
      which fires us,
   Speaks to our hearts and sets our souls
      ablaze,

Teaches and trains, rebukes us and inspires
      us,
   Lord of the Word, receive your people's
      praise.

3 Lord, for our land, in this our generation,
   Spirits oppressed by pleasure, wealth and
      care;
   For young and old, for commonwealth
      and nation,
   Lord of our land, be pleased to hear our
      prayer.

4 Lord, for our world, when men disown
      and doubt him,
   Loveless in strength, and comfortless in
      pain;
   Hungry and helpless, lost indeed without
      him,
   Lord of the world, we pray that Christ
      may reign.

5 Lord, for ourselves; in living power remake
      us —
   Self on the cross and Christ upon the
      throne —
   Past put behind us, for the future take us,
   Lord of our lives, to live for Christ alone.

Timothy Dudley-Smith (1926–)

95 THE ARMOUR OF GOD

1 Lord, we would put around ourselves
   The girding belt of truth:
   This would we put around ourselves,
   A challenge to our youth.

2 Lord, we would wear as coat of mail
   Our trust in what is right:
   This would we wear as coat of mail,
   Our safeguard in the fight.

3 Lord, we would put upon our feet
   The Gospel's shoes of peace:
   These would we put upon our feet
   Until our journeyings cease.

4 Lord, for our shield we take the faith
   That stops the fiery dart:
   This is the shield we take, the faith
   To foil the Tempter's art.

5 Lord, we would put upon our heads
   Your helmet's saving power:
   This would we put upon our heads
   And own it every hour.

6 Lord, we would carry at our side
   Your Spirit's shining sword:
   This would we carry at our side
   The shining Word of God.

7 This would we put upon ourselves
   Complete in every part,
   Careful to wear it constantly:
   The armour of our God.

Cyril G. Hambly (1931–)

96 SO IS MY LORD TO ME

1 As water to the thirsty,
   As beauty to the eyes,
   As strength that follows weakness,
   As truth instead of lies,
   As songtime and springtime
   And summertime to be,
   So is my Lord,
   My living Lord,
   So is my Lord to me.

2 Like calm in place of clamour,
   Like peace that follows pain,
   Like meeting after parting,
   Like sunshine after rain,
   Like moonlight and starlight
   And sunlight on the sea,
   So is my Lord,
   My living Lord,
   So is my Lord to me.

3 A sleep that follows fever,
   As gold instead of grey,
   As freedom after bondage,
   As sunrise to the day,
   As home to the traveller
   And all he longs to see,
   So is my Lord,
   My living Lord,
   So is my Lord to me.

Timothy Dudley-Smith (1926–)

97 TRAVELLING WITH GOD

1 One more step along the world I go,
   One more step along the world I go.
   From the old things to the new
   Keep me travelling along with you.
   And it's from the old I travel to the new.
   Keep me travelling along with you.

2 Round the corner of the world I turn,
   More and more about the world I learn.
   All the new things that I see
   You'll be looking at along with me.
   CHORUS

3 As I travel through the bad and good
   Keep me travelling the way I should.
   Where I see no way to go
   You'll be telling me the way, I know.
   CHORUS

4 Give me courage when the world is rough,
   Keep me loving though the world is tough.
   Leap and sing in all I do,
   Keep me travelling along with you.
   CHORUS

5 You are older than the world can be,
   You are younger than the life in me.
   Ever old and ever new,
   Keep me travelling along with you.
   CHORUS

Sydney Carter (1915–)

98 HELPING EACH OTHER

1 Hands to work and feet to run —
   God's good gifts to me and you;
   Hands and feet he gave to us
   To help each other the whole day through.

2 Eyes to see and ears to hear —
   God's good gifts to me and you;
   Eyes and ears he gave to us
   To help each other the whole day through.

3 Minds to think and hearts to love —
   God's good gifts to me and you;
   Minds and hearts he gave to us
   To help each other the whole day through.

Hilda M. Dodd

99 KIND HANDS

1 Jesus' hands were kind hands, doing good
   to all,
  Healing pain and sickness, blessing
    children small;
  Washing tired feet, and saving those who
    fall;
  Jesus' hands were kind hands, doing good
   to all.

2 Take my hands, Lord Jesus, let them work
   for you,
  Make them strong and gentle, kind in all I
   do;
  Let me watch you, Jesus, till I'm gentle
   too,
  Till my hands are kind hands, quick to
   work for you.

Margaret Cropper (1886–)

100 DISCIPLESHIP

Luke 5, 1 – 11

1 Lord, when you singled out the Three,
  That day of days, by Galilee,
  They did not ask or know
  Exactly what 'to follow' meant,
  To what new aims they gave assent,
  Or where they had to go.

2 In simple faith they followed you
  Because, instinctively, they knew
  Whom they could love and trust;
  And risked the future for your sake,
  And trod the road you had to take,
  As all disciples must.

3 So, when we meet you on that shore,
  And hear your voice demanding more
  Than we had thought to give:
  Then may we know, as they once knew
  Beyond all doubt, that following you
  Is how we want to live.

Fred Pratt Green (1903–)

101 GOD'S FAMILY

1 We must learn to play together,
  For we're all God's family.
  Mustn't fight but play together,
  For we're all God's family.

  Play together,
  Share together,
  Help together,
  Love together,
  For we're all God's family,
  For we're all God's family.

2 We must learn to share together,
  For we're all God's family.
  Mustn't be mean but share together,
  For we're all God's family.
  CHORUS

3 We must learn to help together,
  For we're all God's family.
  Mustn't be lazy but help together,
  For we're all God's family.
  CHORUS

4 We must learn to love together,
  For we're all God's family,
  Mustn't be unkind but love together,
  For we're all God's family.
  CHORUS

Cynthia Raza

102 SING FOR JESUS

  Sing life, sing love, sing Jesus,
  Sing out wherever you are;
  Sing life, sing love, sing Jesus,
  Sing out whoever you are.

1 Life is a gift we can use or abuse,
  Life can be great or a bore.
  It all depends on the way that we choose,
  Whether we notice or just ignore
  God's love.
  CHORUS

2 Love is something we can give or can take.
  Love can bring life or bring death.
  I can love myself and be on the make,
  Or live for others till my last breath
  Like Jesus.
  CHORUS

3 Jesus gives life and in love Jesus died,
  Jesus the Truth and the Way.
  And although he is betrayed and denied,
  In men his life and love live on
  Today.
  CHORUS

Peter Lewis (1940–)

103 LORD OF ALL

1 Christ is the Lord of the smallest atom,
  Christ is the Lord of outer space,
  Christ is the Lord of the constellations,
  Christ is the Lord of every place;
  Of the furthest star,
  Of the coffee bar,
  Of the concrete urban sprawl;
  Of the village green,
  Of the Asian scene,
  Christ is the Lord of all:
  Christ is the Lord of the human heartbeat,
  Christ is the Lord of every breath,
  Christ is the Lord of a man's existence,
  Christ is the Lord of life and death.

2 Christ is the Lord of our thoughts and
      feelings,
  Christ is the Lord of all we plan,
  Christ is the Lord of a man's decision,
  Christ is the Lord of a total man;
  In the local street,
  Where the people meet,
  In the church or a nearby hall;
  In the factory,
  In the family,
  Christ is the Lord of all,
  Christ is the Lord of our love and courtship
  Christ is the Lord of man and wife,
  Christ is the Lord of the things we care for,
  Christ is the Lord of our life.

Kenneth Preston (1916–)

104 THE MAN FOR OTHERS

1 We find thee, Lord, in others' need,
  We seek thee in our brothers;
  By loving word and kindly deed
  We serve the Man for others.

2 We look around and see thy face
  Disfigured, marred, neglected;
  We find thee, Lord, in ev'ry place,
  Sought for and unexpected.

3 We offer in simplicity
  Our loving gift and labour;
  And what we do, we do to thee,
  Incarnate in our neighbour.

4 We love since we are loved by thee;
  New strength from thee we gather;
  And in thy service we shall be
  Made perfect with each other.

Giles Ambrose (1912–)

105 FORGIVENESS

1 'Forgive our sins as we forgive',
  You taught us, Lord, to pray,
  But you alone can grant us grace
  To live the words we say.

2 How can your pardon reach and bless
  The unforgiving heart
  That broods on wrongs and will not let
  Old bitterness depart?

3 In blazing light your Cross reveals
  The truth we dimly knew,
  How small the debts men owe to us,
  How great our debt to you!

4 Lord, cleanse the depths within our souls
  And bid resentment cease;
  Then, reconciled to God and man,
  Our lives will spread your peace.

Rosamond Herklots (1905–)

106 THE NEED OF PRAYER

*It's me, it's me, O Lord, standing in the
      need of prayer;
It's me, it's me, O Lord, standing in the
      need of prayer.*

1 Not my brother nor my sister but it's me,
      O Lord,
  Standing in the need of prayer;
  Not my brother nor my sister but it's me,
      O Lord,
  Standing in the need of prayer.
  CHORUS

2 Not my mother nor my father but it's me,
      O Lord,
  Standing in the need of prayer;
  Not my mother nor my father but it's me,
      O Lord,
  Standing in the need of prayer.
  CHORUS

3 Not the preacher nor my leader but it's me,
O Lord,
Standing in the need of prayer;
Not the preacher nor my leader but it's me,
O Lord,
Standing in the need of prayer.
CHORUS

4 Not the stranger nor my neighbour but it's
me, O Lord,
Standing in the need of prayer;
Not the stranger nor my neighbour but it's
me, O Lord,
Standing in the need of prayer.
CHORUS

*Negro spiritual adapted Peter D. Smith
(1938–)*

107 REGULAR PRAYERTIME

1 Prepare before you pray to God,
Think what you need to say;
Lest holiest of interviews
Is time frittered away.

2 And listen when you pray to God
To what he has to say;
Or dialogue is monologue,
True prayer must be two-way.

3 Be silent when you pray to God,
Tongue tied to find the word;
In grief, anxiety or doubt,
Your prayer's already heard.

Bernard Braley (1924–)

108 PRAYER OF ST FRANCIS

1 Make me a channel of your peace.
Where there is hatred, let me bring your
love;
Where there is injury, your pardon, Lord;
And where there's doubt, true faith in you.
*Oh, Master, grant that I may never seek
So much to be consoled as to console;
To be understood as to understand;
To be loved, as to love with all my soul.*

2 Make me a channel of your peace.
Where there's despair in life let me bring
hope;
Where there is darkness, only light;
And where there's sadness, ever joy.
CHORUS

3 Make me a channel of your peace.
It is in pardoning that we are pardoned,
In giving to all men that we receive;
And in dying that we're born to eternal
life.

Saint Francis (1182-1226)

109 LIVING LORD

**Verse 2 should only be sung
when Holy Communion is being celebrated*

1 Lord Jesus Christ,
You have come to us,
You are one with us,
Mary's Son.
Cleansing our souls from all their sin,
Pouring your love and goodness in,
Jesus, our love for you we sing,
Living Lord.

*2 Lord Jesus Christ,
Now and every day
Teach us how to pray,
Son of God.
You have commanded us to do
This, in remembrance, Lord, of you:
Into our lives your power breaks through,
Living Lord.

3 Lord Jesus Christ,
You have come to us,
Born as one of us,
Mary's Son.
Led out to die on Calvary,
Risen from death to set us free,
Living Lord Jesus, help us see
You are Lord.

4 Lord Jesus Christ,
I would come to you,
Live my life for you,
Son of God.
All your commands I know are true,
Your many gifts will make me new,
Into my life your power breaks through,
Living Lord.

Patrick Appleford (1925–)

110 CHRIST THE WORKMAN

1 Lord, look upon our working days,
  Busied in factory, office, store;
  May wordless work your name adore,
  The common round spell out your praise.

2 Bent to the lot our crafts assign,
  Swayed by deep tides of need and fear,
  In loyalties torn the truth unclear,
  How may we build to your design?

3 You are the workman, Lord, not we:
  All worlds were made at your command,
  Christ, their sustainer, bared his hand,
  Retrieved them from futility.

4 Our part to do what he'll commit,
  Who strides the world, and calls men all
  Partners in pain and carnival,
  To grasp the hope he won for it.

5 Cover our faults with pardon full,
  Shield those who suffer when we shirk:
  Take what is worthy in our work,
  Give it its portion in your rule.

Ian M. Fraser (1917–)

111 MOTHER TERESA'S DAILY PRAYER

1 Make us worthy, Lord,
  Make us worthy, Lord,
  To serve our fellow men,
  To serve our fellow men.
  Make us worthy, Lord,
  Make us worthy, Lord,
  To serve our fellow men,
  To serve our fellow men
  Throughout the world who live and die,
  Throughout the world who live and die
  In poverty and hunger,
  In poverty and hunger.
  Ah, Ah, la la la la la la la, Ah, Ah.

2 Give them through our hands,
  Give them through our hands
  This day, their daily bread,
  This day, their daily bread.
  Give them, through our hands,
  Give them, through our hands,

This day, their daily bread,
  This day, their daily bread,
  And by our understanding love,
  And by our understanding love
  Give peace and joy,
  Give peace and joy.
  Ah, Ah, la la la la la la la, Ah, Ah.

Traditional

112 A MATURE FAITH

1 When our confidence is shaken
  In beliefs we thought secure;
  When the spirit in its sickness
  Seeks but cannot find a cure:
  God is active in the tensions
  Of a faith not yet mature.

2 Solar systems, void of meaning,
  Freeze the spirit into stone;
  Always our researches lead us
  To the ultimate Unknown:
  Faith must die, or come full circle
  To its source in God alone.

3 In the discipline of praying,
  When it's hardest to believe;
  In the drudgery of caring,
  When it's not enough to grieve:
  Faith, maturing, learns acceptance
  Of the insights we receive.

4 God is love; and he redeems us
  In the Christ we crucify;
  This is God's eternal answer
  To mankind's eternal Why:
  May we in this faith maturing
  Be content to live and die!

Fred Pratt Green (1903–)

113 LIVE IN US!

1 All who worship God in Jesus, all who
      serve the Son of Man
  In the Kingdom he prepared for us before
      the world began,
  Are committed to his purpose in the
      things we do and plan.
  Lord Jesus, live in us!

2 When the forces that divide us threaten all
    that God has made,
  When it's easy to find reasons why the
    truth should be betrayed:
  We who bear the name of Christian, we
    know who must be obeyed.
  Lord Jesus, live in us!

3 It's his deeper revolution which redeems
    us when we fall;
  It's his reconciling spirit shall make
    comrades of us all;
  It's the joy of God within us cries in
    answer to his call:
  Lord Jesus, live in us!
  Live in me!

Fred Pratt Green (1903–)

114 PARTNERS IN SERVICE

1 Father, help your people
  In this world to build
  Something of your Kingdom,
  And to do your will.
  Lead us to discover
  Partnership in love;
  Bless our ways of sharing,
  And our pride reprove.

2 Lord of desk and altar,
  Bind our lives in one,
  That in work and worship
  Love may set the tone.
  Give us grace to listen,
  Clarity of speech.
  Make us truly thankful
  For the gifts of each.

3 Holy is the setting
  Of each room and yard,
  Lecture hall and kitchen,
  Office, shop and ward.
  Holy is the rhythm
  Of our working hours;
  Hallow then our purpose,
  Energy and powers.

4 Strengthen, Lord, for service
  Hand and heart and brain;
  Help us good relations
  Daily to maintain.
  Let the loving presence
  Of the servant-Christ
  Heighten our devotion,
  Make our life a feast.

Fred Kaan (1929–)

115 THE WAY, THE TRUTH AND THE LIFE

1 He is the Way, the end of all my searching:
  He is the Truth: I'll trust his every word;
  He is the Life abundant, everlasting:
  This is the Christ, the Saviour of the world.

2 More of the Way, dear Lord, be this my
    choosing:
  More of the Truth, Lord, teach me day by
    day:
  More of the Life, for ever satisfying:
  More of thyself, the Life, the Truth, the
    Way!

G. Brattle

116 THE WAY

1 When you are angry and feel you've been
    wronged,
  Listen to what he would say:
  'Learn to forgive, as God forgives you.'
  Seeking and saving, he shows us the way,
  Seeking and saving, he shows us the way.

2 When you feel hatred and want to strike out,
  Listen to what he would say:
  'Love your opponents, seek good for your
    foes.'
  Living and loving he shows us the way,
  Living and loving he shows us the way.

3 When you're in pain and the future seems
    dim,
  Listen to what he would say:
  'Trust me to give you fulfilment and
    peace.'
  Teaching and healing he shows us the way,
  Teaching and healing he shows us the way.

4 When you feel lost and that life's passed
    you by,
  Listen to what he would say:
  'Come to the Father, he cares for you
    still.'
  Dying and rising, he shows us the way,
  Dying and rising, he shows us the way.

Peter D. Smith (1938–)

117 GOD IS MY STRENGTH

1 I lift my eyes
  To the quiet hills
  In the press of a busy day;
  As green hills stand
  In a dusty land
  So God is my strength and stay.

2 I lift my eyes
  To the quiet hills
  To a calm that is mine to share;
  Secure and still
  In the Father's will
  And kept by the Father's care.

3 I lift my eyes
  To the quiet hills
  With a prayer as I turn to sleep;
  By day, by night,
  Through the dark and light
  My Shepherd will guard his sheep.

4 I lift me eyes
  To the quiet hills
  And my heart to the Father's throne;
  In all my ways
  To the end of days
  The Lord will preserve his own.

Timothy Dudley-Smith (1926–)

118 THE PRAISE OF OUR HANDS

Praise the Lord, all the work of our hands,
Serve him, reveal him in all we do.

1 Fingers trimming, knitting, sewing,
  Muscles busy digging, hoeing,
  Look at how our skills are growing,
  Serve him, reveal him in all we do.
  CHORUS

2 Fixing engines, house repairing,
  Washing, rinsing, drying, airing,
  For our families we are caring,
  Serve him, reveal him in all we do.
  CHORUS

3 Flower arranging, painting, baking,
  Furniture and curtain making,
  Work well done though arms are aching,
  Serve him, reveal him in all we do.
  CHORUS

4 Hands extended clasped in greeting,
  Hands held tight in lovers' meeting,
  'Make it up!' say hands, entreating,
  Serve him, reveal him in all we do.
  CHORUS

Bernard Braley (1924–)

CHURCH

AND COMMUNITY

in which we sing of the
Holy Spirit and the Church,
provide hymns for the sacraments
of Baptism and Holy Communion,
and consider the role of the
Church as servant.

Recommended hymns from standard books

119 THE CONTEMPORARY CHURCH

1 God of grace and God of glory,
  On thy people pour thy power;
  Crown thine ancient Church's story;
  Bring her bud to glorious flower.
  Grant us wisdom,
  Grant us courage,
  For the facing of this hour.

2 Lo! the hosts of evil round us
  Scorn thy Christ, assail his ways!
  Fears and doubts too long have bound us;
  Free our hearts to work and praise.
  Grant us wisdom,
  Grant us courage,
  For the living of these days.

3 Heal thy children's warring madness;
  Bend our pride to thy control;
  Shame our wanton, selfish gladness,
  Rich in things and poor in soul.
  Grant us wisdom,
  Grant us courage,
  Lest we miss thy Kingdom's goal.

4 Set our feet on lofty places;
  Gird our lives that they may be
  Armoured with all Christ-like graces
  In the fight to set men free.
  Grant us wisdom,
  Grant us courage,
  That we fail not man nor thee.

H.E. Fosdick (1878–1972)

120 THE FIRE OF PENTECOST

1 Like fireworks lighting up the night
  The Holy Spirit came:
  Dejected Christians felt the touch
  Of living fronds of flame —
  And suddenly, the world was young
  And nothing looked the same.

2 For Jesus' nearness gave them heart
  To venture, come what would:
  The love of Jesus bade them share
  Their house, possessions, food:
  The mind of Jesus gave them speech
  That all men understood.

3 This is the Spirit who today
  Our daring will inspire
  And common folk are given gifts
  To change the world entire:
  The sparks which flew at Pentecost
  Began a forest fire.

Ian M. Fraser (1917–)

121 PENTECOST

1 We went with a message
  And got them to hear it,
  The day that the Spirit
  Took over our lives.

2 He came in a wind that
  Went over and through us,
  That lifted and blew us
  And whirled us outside;
  He set us on fire and
  We had to declare it,
  The day that the Spirit
  Came down as our Guide.

3 He filled us with courage
  That nothing could smother,
  They looked at each other
  And blamed it on wine.
  But that was a sneer we
  Did nothing to merit
  The day that the Spirit
  Performed his design.

4 They shouted us down and
  They put us in prison,
  But still had to listen
  And not shut their ears.
  As Jesus had said, we
  Were able to bear it
  The day that the Spirit
  Disposed of our fears.

5 And why are we talking,
  Who live in the present,
  As if we were present
  That famous Third Hour?
  Why! We are their brothers,
  Entitled to share it —
  The day that the Spirit
  Exploded in power.

Michael Hewlett (1916–)

122 WHITSUN CANTICLE

I will pour out my Spirit on all flesh,
Your sons and your daughters shall
  prophesy,
Your old men shall dream dreams
And your young men shall see visions.

1 I will pray the Father and he will give you
    another Counsellor to be with you for
    ever.
  When the Spirit of Truth comes he will
    guide you into all the truth.
  CHORUS

2 The Counsellor, the Holy Spirit, whom the
    Father will send in my name,
  He will teach you all things, bring to
    remembrance all that I have said to
    you.
  CHORUS

3 And suddenly a sound came from heaven
    like the rush of a mighty wind
  And it filled the house where they were
    sitting and they were all filled with
    the Holy Spirit.
  CHORUS

4 Likewise the Spirit helps us in our
    weakness for we do not know how to
    pray as we ought;
  But the Spirit himself intercedes for us
    with sighs too deep for words.
  CHORUS

Adapted by Alan Luff (1928–) from Revised
Standard Version of the Bible

123 OBEYING THE SPIRIT

1 I'm gonna sing when the Spirit says 'Sing',
  I'm gonna sing when the Spirit says 'Sing',
  I'm gonna sing when the Spirit says 'Sing',
  And obey the Spirit of the Lord.

2 I'm gonna love when the Spirit says 'Love',
  I'm gonna love when the Spirit says 'Love',
  I'm gonna love when the Spirit says 'Love',
  And obey the Spirit of the Lord.

3 I'm gonna laugh when the Spirit says
   'Laugh',
  I'm gonna laugh when the Spirit says
   'Laugh',
  I'm gonna laugh when the Spirit says
   'Laugh',
  And obey the Spirit of the Lord.

4 I'm gonna heal when the Spirit says 'Heal',
  I'm gonna heal when the Spirit says 'Heal',
  I'm gonna heal when the Spirit says 'Heal',
  And obey the Spirit of the Lord.

5 I'm gonna hope when the Spirit says
   'Hope',
  I'm gonna hope when the Spirit says
   'Hope',
  I'm gonna hope when the Spirit says
   'Hope',
  And obey the Spirit of the Lord.

6 I'm gonna care when the Spirit says 'Care',
  I'm gonna care when the Spirit says 'Care',
  I'm gonna care when the Spirit says 'Care',
  And obey the Spirit of the Lord.

7 I'm gonna give when the Spirit says 'Give',
  I'm gonna give when the Spirit says 'Give',
  I'm gonna give when the Spirit says 'Give',
  And obey the Spirit of the Lord.

8 I'm gonna trust when the Spirit says
   'Trust',
  I'm gonna trust when the Spirit says
   'Trust',
  I'm gonna trust when the Spirit says
   'Trust',
  And obey the Spirit of the Lord.

9 I'm gonna bless when the Spirit says
   'Bless',
  I'm gonna bless when the Spirit says
   'Bless',
  I'm gonna bless when the Spirit says
   'Bless',
  And obey the Spirit of the Lord.

10 I'm gonna seek when the Spirit says 'Seek',
  I'm gonna seek when the Spirit says 'Seek',
  I'm gonna seek when the Spirit says 'Seek',
  And obey the Spirit of the Lord.

Traditional adapted Peter D. Smith (1938–)

124 GOD'S HOLY SPIRIT

1 Upon the Day of Pentecost
  The Holy Spirit came –
  Like powerful, rushing, mighty wind
  And leaping, living flame.

2 The friends of Jesus till that hour
  Were fearful folk and weak;
  But now the Holy Spirit made
  Them bold and wise to speak.

3 With joy and confidence they went
  To all whom they could reach,
  In God the Holy Spirit's power
  To praise and heal and teach.

4 God's Holy Spirit still is here
  To guide our world today,
  And helps the friends of Jesus Christ
  In what they do and say.

Patricia Hunt (1921–)

125 THE SPIRIT'S POWER TODAY

1 There's a spirit in the air,
  Telling Christians everywhere:
  'Praise the love that Christ revealed,
  Living, working in our world'.

2 Lose your shyness, find your tongue,
  Tell the world what God has done:
  God in Christ has come to stay.
  We can see his power today.

3 When believers break the bread,
  When a hungry child is fed,
  Praise the love that Christ revealed,
  Living, working, in our world.

4 Still his Spirit leads the fight,
  Seeing wrong and setting right:
  God in Christ has come to stay.
  We can see his power today.

5 When a stranger's not alone,
  Where the homeless find a home,
  Praise the love that Christ revealed,
  Living, working, in our world.

6 May his Spirit fill our praise,
  Guide our thoughts and change our ways.
  God in Christ has come to stay.
  We can see his power today.

7 There's a Spirit in the air,
   Calling people everywhere:
   'Praise the love that Christ revealed,
   Living, working, in our world'.

Brian A. Wren (1936–)

126 CHURCH METAPHORS

1 We are of that honoured company
   Called to be the Church of Christ;
   One with the saints of old,
   Firmly their truth to hold,
   Here to bear the lamp of faith for all to
      see.

2 We are of that blithe and happy throng
   Called the Bride of Christ our Lord;
   Sought from his home above,
   Held with undying love,
   Nought can take us from his side where we
      belong.

3 We are of that green and fruitful wood
   Called the branches of the Vine;
   Nourished by Jesus' care,
   Purged, the best fruit to bear,
   Staying at the source of our eternal food.

4 We are of that present active band
   Called the Body of our Lord;
   Members incorporate,
   Each to participate,
   Sharing in the work of love that he has
      planned.

Cyril G. Hambly (1931–)

127 THE CHURCH OF CHRIST

1 God is here! As we his People
   Meet to offer praise and prayer,
   May we find in fuller measure
   What it is in Christ we share.
   Here, as in the world around us,
   All our varied skills and arts
   Wait the coming of his Spirit
   Into open minds and hearts.

2 Here are symbols to remind us
   Of our lifelong need of grace;
   Here are table, font, and pulpit;
   Here the cross has central place.
   Here in honesty of preaching,
   Here in silence, as in speech,
   Here, in newness and renewal,
   God the Spirit comes to each.

3 Here our children find a welcome
   In the Shepherd's flock and fold,
   Here, as bread and wine are taken,
   Christ sustains us, as of old.
   Here the servants of the Servant
   Seek in worship to explore
   What it means in daily living
   To believe and to adore.

4 Lord of all, of Church and Kingdom,
   In an age of change and doubt,
   Keep us faithful to the Gospel,
   Help us work your purpose out.
   Here, in this day's dedication,
   All we have to give, receive:
   We, who cannot live without you,
   We adore you! We believe!

Fred Pratt Green (1903–)

128 THE PEOPLE OF GOD

1 'Moses I know you're the man,'
   The Lord said.
   'You're going to work out my plan,'
   The Lord said.
   'Lead all the Israelites out of slavery,
   And I shall make them a wandering race
   Called the People of God.'
   So every day,
   We're on our way,
   For we're a travelling, wandering race,
   We're the People of God.

2 'Don't get too set in your ways,'
   The Lord said.
   'Each step is only a phase,'
   The Lord said.
   'I'll go before you and I shall be a sign
   To guide my travelling, wandering race,
   You're the People of God.'
   CHORUS

3 'No matter what you may do,'
   The Lord said,
   'I shall be faithful and true,'
   The Lord said,
   'My love will strengthen you as you go
      along,
   For you're my travelling, wandering race,
   You're the People of God.'
   CHORUS

4 'Look at the birds in the air,'
   The Lord said,
   'They fly unhampered by care,'
   The Lord said,
   'You will move easier if you're travelling
      light,
   For you're a wandering, vagabond race,
   You're the People of God.'
   CHORUS

5 'Foxes have places to go,'
   The Lord said,
   'But I've no home here below,'
   The Lord said,
   'So if you want to be with me all your days,
   Keep up the moving and travelling on,
   You're the People of God.'
   CHORUS

Estelle White (1925–)

129 TOMORROW'S DAY

1 Now let us from this table rise
   Renewed in body, mind and soul;
   With Christ we die and live again,
   His selfless love has made us whole.

2 With minds alert, upheld by grace,
   To spread the Word in speech and deed,
   We follow in the steps of Christ,
   At one with man in hope and need.

3 To fill each human house with love,
   It is the sacrament of care;
   The work that Christ began to do
   We humbly pledge ourselves to share.

4 Then grant us courage, Father God,
   To choose again the pilgrim way
   And help us to accept with joy
   The challenge of tomorrow's day.

Fred Kaan (1929–)

130 OUR COMMON BREAD

1 As we break the bread
   And taste the life of wine,
   We bring to mind our Lord,
   Man of all time.

2 Grain is sown to die;
   It rises from the dead,
   Becomes through human toil
   Our common bread.

3 Pass from hand to hand
   The living love of Christ!
   Machine and man provide
   Bread for this feast.

4 Jesus binds in one
   Our daily life and work;
   He is of all mankind
   Symbol and mark.

5 Having shared the bread
   That died to rise again,
   We rise to serve the world,
   Scattered as grain.

Fred Kaan (1929–)

131 LET US BREAK BREAD TOGETHER

1 Let us break bread together on our knees;
   Let us break bread together on our knees:
   When I fall on my knees,
   With my face to the rising sun,
   O Lord, have mercy on me.

2 Let us drink wine together on our knees;
   Let us drink wine together on our knees:
   CHORUS

3 Let us praise God together on our knees;
   Let us praise God together on our knees:
   CHORUS

Negro spiritual

132 THE LAST SUPPER

1 'Where shall we get ready the meal?'
   The friends came to Jesus and asked.
   He said, 'Go to the city,
   A man carries water,
   You follow him into his house.'
   And they did what he said,
   They did what he said,
   'You follow him into his house.'
   And they did what he said,
   They did what he said,
   'You follow him into his house.'

2 They spoke to the man of the house,
 'Now Jesus is needing a room.'
 He said, 'Up on the house top
 A room, chairs and table,
 And there you'll get ready the meal.'
 And they did what he said,
 They did what he said,
 'And there you'll get ready the meal.'
 And they did what he said,
 They did what he said,
 'And there you'll get ready the meal.'

3 And Jesus broke bread with his hands,
 And passed it to each of his friends.
 He said, 'Take it and share it,
 For you it is broken,
 Remember me when you eat bread.'
 And they did what he said,
 They did what he said,
 Remembered him when they ate bread.
 And they did what he said,
 They did what he said,
 Remembered him when they ate bread.

4 Then Jesus took wine in a cup,
 He passed it to each of his friends.
 He said, 'Take it and share it,
 For you I will pour it,
 Remember me when you drink wine.'
 And they did what he said,
 They did what he said,
 Remembered him when they drank wine.
 And they did what he said,
 They did what he said,
 Remembered him when they drank wine.

John Tearnan (1937–)

133 BRING BREAD, BRING WINE!

1 Reap me the earth as a harvest to God,
 Gather and bring it again,
 All that is his, to the Maker of all.
 Lift it and offer it high:
 Bring bread, bring wine,
 Give glory to the Lord.
 Whose is the earth but God's,
 Whose is the praise but his?

2 Go with your song and your music, with
  joy,
 Go to the altar of God.
 Carry your offerings, fruits of the earth,
 Work of your labouring hands:
 CHORUS

3 Gladness and pity and passion and pain,
 All that is mortal in man,
 Lay all before him, return him his gift,
 God, to whom all shall go home:
 CHORUS

Peter Icarus

134 BAPTISM - 1

1 Lord Jesus, once a child,
 Saviour of young and old,
 Receive this little child of ours
 Into your flock and fold.

2 You drank the cup of life,
 It's bitterness and bliss,
 And loved us to the uttermost
 For such a child as this.

3 So help us, Lord, to trust,
 Through this baptismal rite,
 Not in our own imperfect love,
 But in your saving might.

4 Lord Jesus, for his (her) sake,
 Lend us your constant aid,
 That he (she), when older, may rejoice
 We kept the vows we made.

Fred Pratt Green (1903–)

135 BAPTISM - 2

1 Lord, you give to us
 The precious gift of life,
 A stewardship for every husband, every
  wife.

2 Lord, you give to us
 Not only flesh and blood,
 But mind and heart and soul to know that
  they are good.

3 Lord, you offer us
 The water, bread and wine.
 By faith we reach out for your love within
  the sign.

4 Lord, you offer us
 New life that never ends –
 You suffer, serve, and die, and live to call
  us friends.

5 Lord, you ask of us
    A death to what we knew.
    Then, rising in your name, we'll put our
        trust in you.

6 Lord, you share with us
    Our hope for what will be.
    With us prepare each child by love, your
        love to see.

Stephen Orchard (1942–)

136 A GIFT OF A CHILD

1 This child from God above,
    The Father's gift divine –
    To this new life of light and love
    We give his seal and sign:

2 To bear the eternal Name,
    To walk the Master's way,
    The Father's covenant to claim,
    The Spirit's will obey;

3 To take the Saviour's Cross,
    In faith to hold it fast;
    And for it reckon all things loss
    As long as life shall last;

4 To tell his truth abroad,
    To tread the path he trod,
    With all who love and serve the Lord –
    The family of God.

Timothy Dudley-Smith (1926–)

137 A HYMN FOR MOTHERING SUNDAY

1 How great the debt we owe
    To those who love us most;
    They give us birth, and help us grow,
    And rarely count the cost.

2 To make us feel secure
    They lose their life in ours;
    And what they mean to us is more
    Than we can say with flowers.

3 How can we measure love?
    Yet treasure it we must,
    For what God gives us from above
    Is held by us in trust.

4 Then let us vow today,
    As those who know love's worth,
    To love, to worship, and obey
    The Lord of all the earth.

Fred Pratt Green (1903–)

138 BROTHERHOOD IN CHRIST

1 In Christ there is no East or West,
    In him no South or North,
    But one great fellowship of love
    Throughout the whole wide earth.

2 In him shall true hearts everywhere
    Their high communion find,
    His service is the golden cord
    Close-binding all mankind.

3 Join hands, then, brothers of the Faith,
    What'er your race may be;
    Who serves my Father as a son
    Is surely kin to me.

4 In Christ now meet both East and West,
    In him meet South and North,
    All Christlike souls are one in him,
    Throughout the whole wide earth.

John Oxenham (1852-1941)

139 THE BODY OF CHRIST

1 We are the Body of Christ,
    Let us be one.
    We are the Body of Christ
    And there's work to be done.

2 We are the People of God,
    Let us unite.
    We are the People of God
    And we live in his light.

3 We are the limbs of the Lord,
    Help us to move.
    We are the limbs of the Lord
    As our actions will approve.

4 We have the power of God,
    His Spirit's here.
    We have the power of God
    And we've nothing to fear.

5 We are the Body of Christ,
    Let us be one.
    We are the Body of Christ
    And there's work to be done.

Ken Okines (1946–)

140 CONFIRMATION AND COMMITMENT

1 Lord, we have come at your own
     invitation,
 Chosen by you, to be counted your
     friends;
 Yours is the strength that sustains
     dedication,
 Ours a commitment we know never ends.

2 Here, at your table, confirm our
     intention,
 Give it your seal of forgiveness and grace;
 Teach us to serve, without pride or
     pretension,
 Lord, in your Kingdom, whatever our
     place.

3 When, at your table, each time of
     returning,
 Vows are renewed and our courage
     restored:
 May we increasingly glory in learning
 All that it means to accept you as Lord.

4 So, in the world, where each duty assigned
     us
 Gives us the chance to create or destroy,
 Help us to make those decisions that bind
     us,
 Lord, to yourself, in obedience and joy.

Fred Pratt Green (1903–)

141 SPIRIT OF THE LIVING GOD

 Spirit of the living God,
 Fall afresh on me.
 Spirit of the living God,
 Fall fresh on me.
 Break me, melt me, mould me, fill me
 Spirit of the living God,
 Fall afresh on me.

Daniel Iverson

142 MAKE US ONE

1 Lord Christ, the Father's mighty Son,
 Whose work upon the Cross was done
 All men to receive,
 Make all our scattered churches one,
 That the world may believe.

2 To make us one your prayers were said,
 To make us one you broke the bread
 For all to receive;
 Its pieces scatter us instead:
 How can others believe?

3 Lord Christ, forgive us, make us new!
 What our designs could never do
 Your love can achieve.
 Our prayers, our work, we bring to you,
 That the world may believe.

Brian A. Wren (1936–)

143 TELL ALL THE WORLD

1 Shout it in the street,
 Tell it to your friend,
 Spread it through the earth from end to
     end,
 Go to every people,
 Tell them all to come,
 For the Spirit of God shall make us one.

2 Listen to the world,
 Listen in your room,
 Listen for his call come late or soon,
 Ready for adventure,
 Following his will,
 For the Spirit of God shall lead us still.

Edmund Banyard (1920–)

144 LIGHT UP THE FIRE

1 Colours of the day dawn into the mind,
 The day has begun, the night is behind.
 Go down to the city, into the street,
 And let's give the message to the people
     we meet.
 So light up the fire and let the flame burn,
 Open the door, let Jesus return,
 Take seeds of his Spirit, let the fruit grow,
 Tell the people of Jesus,
 Let his love show.

2 Go through the park, on into the town,
 The sun still shines on, it never goes down:
 The Light of the World is risen again,
 The people of darkness are needing our
     Friend.
 CHORUS

3 Open your eyes, look into the sky,
The darkness has come, the sun came to
die.
The evening draws on, the sun disappears,
But Jesus is living, his Spirit is near.
CHORUS

McLelland, Pac and Rycroft

145 THANKSGIVING FOR THE BIBLE

1 Thanks be to God, who has given us our
Bible,
Through each new century guarding his
truth;
Bearing his Word, the eternal evangel:
Comfort of age and a challenge to youth.

2 Poetry; prophecy; treasures of wisdom;
Laws of the ancients; apostles' advice;
Histories; letters; and lives of the Master:
All are contained in this pearl beyond
price.

3 Bless all the scholars who lend us their
learning;
Guide the translators and harness their
skill.
Help us, O God, as we seek for your
meaning;
May all who study it bend to your will.

4 Glory to God for his true revelation,
Ever unfolding, in Jesus complete.
We who are treading the path to his
Kingdom
Find in these pages a light for our feet.

Cyril G. Hambly (1931–)

146 GOD'S WORD

1 The Bible speaks in many tongues
With strange, compelling power,
But does it ring with living truth
In this our modern hour?

2 It tells us of a race that found
Its faith in bygone days,
That suffered much, and learned in part
God's nature and his ways,

3 Till Jesus Christ, the Word made Flesh,
The roads of Israel trod,
Himself the new and living Way
To bring us all to God.

4 Here faintly we begin to trace
One vast and timeless Plan,
God's answer to the mysteries
That haunt the soul of man.

5 If through these pages God would speak
When man's last word is said,
How can we go our heedless way
And leave this book unread?

6 Though much may daunt us as we read,
We'll pray for eyes to see
And hearts to know by full response
The truth that makes us free.

Rosamond Herklots (1905–)

147 THE WORD OF AMOS

1 In affairs of economics
Prophet Amos spoke the Word;
But the men of shop and office
Closed their ears to what they heard;
Money ceased to be a servant,
Means of meeting human need,
Killed the heart of God's own People
Ruled by power of human greed.

2 In affairs of church attendance
Prophet Amos spoke the Word;
But both priests and foolish people
Closed their ears to what they heard:
Worship ceased to be a service
Offered gladly from the heart,
Lacked the sacrificial living,
Its essential other part.

3 In affairs of daily leisure
Prophet Amos spoke the Word;
But the constant background music
Closed their ears to what they heard:
Leisure ceased to be a tonic
Recreating soul and mind,
Men and women drunk with pleasure
Lost the gift of being kind.

4 To the soul of every nation
Prophet Amos speaks the Word;
In our leisure, commerce, worship,
Hear the counsel of the Lord:
Fear the wrath of holy judgement
Self-inflicted by our ways,
Let the will of God Almighty
Be the ruler of our days.

Bernard Braley (1924–)

148 BELONGING

1 As the bridegroom to his chosen,
  As the king unto his realm,
  As the keep unto the castle,
  As the pilot to the helm,
  So, Lord, art thou to me.

2 As the fountain in the garden,
  As the candle in the dark,
  As the treasure in the coffer,
  As the manna in the ark,
  So, Lord, art thou to me.

3 As the music at the banquet,
  As the stamp unto the seal,
  As the medicine to the fainting,
  As the wine-cup at the meal,
  So, Lord, art thou to me.

4 As the ruby in the setting,
  As the honey in the comb,
  As the light within the lantern,
  As the father in the home,
  So, Lord, art thou to me.

5 As the sunshine in the heavens,
  As the image in the glass,
  As the fruit unto the fig-tree,
  As the dew unto the grass,
  So, Lord, art thou to me.

Paraphrased from John Tauler (1300-1361)
by E.F. Bevan (1827-1909)

149 THE FAMILY OF MAN

1 I belong to a family, the biggest on Earth,
  A thousand every day are coming to birth.
  Our name isn't Wilkinson, Davies or Jones,
  It's the name every man should be proud
    he owns:
  It's the family of man, keeps growing,
  The family of man, keeps sowing
  The seeds of a new life every day.

2 I've got a sister in Melbourne, and brother
    in Paree,
  The whole wide world is dad and mother
    to me.
  Wherever you turn you will find my kin,
  Whatever the creed or the colour of skin:
  CHORUS

3 The miner in the Rhondda, the coolie in
    Pekin,
  Men across the world who reap and plough
    and spin,
  They've got a life and others to share it,
  Let's bridge the oceans and declare it:
  CHORUS

4 Some people say the world is a horrible
    place,
  But it's just as good or bad as the human
    race;
  Dirt and misery or health and joy,
  Man can build or can destroy:
  CHORUS

Karl Frederick Dallas

150 THE TIME OF OUR LIFE

1 Thank you, O Lord, for the time that is
    now,
  For all the newness your minutes allow,
  Make us alert with your presence of mind,
  Keep us alive to the claims of mankind.

2 Thank you, O Lord, for the time that is past,
  For all the values and thoughts that will
    last,
  May we all stagnant tradition ignore,
  Leaving behind things that matter no more.

3 Thank you for hopes of the day that will
    come,
  For all the change that will happen in time:
  Lord, for the future our spirits prepare,
  Hallow our doubts and redeem us from
    fear.

4 Make us afraid of the thoughts that delay,
  Faithful in all the affairs of today,
  Keep us, our Father, from playing it safe,
  Thank you that now is the time of our life.

Fred Kaan (1929–)

151 READY AND WILLING

1 When I needed a neighbour, were you there,
    were you there?
  When I needed a neighbour, were you there?
  And the creed and the colour and the name
    won't matter,
  Were you there?

2 I was hungry and thirsty, were you there,
      were you there?
  I was hungry and thirsty, were you there?
  CHORUS

3 I was cold, I was naked, were you there,
      were you there?
  I was cold, I was naked, were you there?
  CHORUS

4 When I needed a shelter, were you there,
      were you there?
  When I needed a shelter, were you there?
  CHORUS

5 When I needed a healer, were you there,
      were you there?
  When I needed a healer, were you there?
  CHORUS

6 Wherever you travel, I'll be there, I'll be
      there,
  Wherever you travel, I'll be there.
  And the creed and the colour and the name
      won't matter,
  I'll be there.

Sydney Carter (1915–)

152 CHRISTIAN AID

1 Once upon a time they went,
  King and page together,
  On a deed of kindness bent,
  In the winter weather.
  Every legend has its truth,
  May this one remind us
  Where a neighbour is in need
  Christ expects to find us.

2 Victims of injustice cry:
  On your own confession
  Charity is not enough,
  We must end oppression.
  Yet, in such a world as this,
  Daily we are proving
  There are evils none can cure
  Without deeds of loving.

3 We must follow in his steps
  Who was found in fashion
  As a man, yet never lost
  His divine compassion.
  Lord, release such love in us,
  We shall be more ready
  To reach out with speedy aid
  To your poor and needy.

Fred Pratt Green (1903–)

153 THE EARTH IS THE LORD'S

1 God of concrete, God of steel,
  God of piston and of wheel,
  God of pylon and of steam,
  God of girder and of beam,
  God of atom, God of mine,
  All the world of power is thine!

2 Lord of cable, Lord of rail,
  Lord of motorway and mail,
  Lord of rocket, Lord of flight,
  Lord of soaring satellite,
  Lord of lightning's livid line,
  All the world of speed is thine!

3 Lord of science, Lord of art,
  God of map and graph and chart,
  Lord of physics and research,
  Word of Bible, Faith of Church,
  Lord of sequence and design,
  All the world of truth is thine!

4 God whose glory fills the earth
  Gave the universe its birth
  Loosed the Christ with Easter's might,
  Saves the world from evil's blight,
  Claims mankind by grace divine,
  All the world of love is thine!

Richard Jones (1926–)

154 BE WITH US!

1 Be at every family table,
  Share the pain in every ward,
  Join the busy shopping precinct,
  Caring, constant, loving Lord,
  Caring, constant, loving Lord.

2 Be at every Union meeting,
  Fill a chair at every Board,
  Join each busy factory's payroll,
  Caring, constant, loving Lord,
  Caring, constant, loving Lord.

3 Be with every nation's leaders,
  Give them grace to seek accord,
  Help them fight with human suffering,
  Caring, constant, loving Lord,
  Caring, constant, loving Lord.

4 Be at every Christian gathering,
  Guide our hearts to do your will;
  Give us power to know your Lordship,
  Caring, constant, loving still,
  Caring, constant, loving still.

5 Be with those who feel rejected,
  Share the lot of those depressed,
  Unemployed, unsure, unwanted,
  Caring, constant, loving Guest,
  Caring, constant, loving Guest.

Bernard Braley (1924–)

155 A PRAYER FOR THE MODERN CITY

1 With clearing skies around us
  And hushed the traffic's noise,
  Increase our city's beauty,
  Restore, O Lord, its joys.
  As older folk, contented,
  Their good companions meet,
  May children, singing, playing,
  Bring laughter to their street.

2 Lord, prosper trade and commerce;
  Our civic life keep pure;
  Our labour and our leisure,
  Our love of home, secure.
  Outside a town, rejected,
  The Lord of life was slain;
  This modern city needs you;
  Stay with us Lord and reign.

Alan Ogle (1922–)

156 A VITAL QUESTION

1 'Am I my brother's keeper?'
  The muttered cry was drowned
  By Abel's life blood shouting
  In silence from the ground.
  For no man is an island
  Divided from the main,
  The bell which tolled for Abel
  Tolled equally for Cain.

2 The ruler called for water
  And thought his hands were clean.
  Christ counted less than order,
  The man than the machine.
  The crowd cried 'Crucify him',
  Their malice wouldn't budge,
  So Pilate called for water,
  And history's his judge.

3 As long as people hunger,
  As long as people thirst,
  And ignorance and illness
  And warfare do their worst,
  As long as there's injustice
  In any of God's lands,
  I am my brother's keeper,
  I dare not wash my hands.

John Ferguson (1921–)

157 GO DOWN, MOSES

1 When Israel was in Egypt's land,
  Let my People go;
  Oppressed so hard they could not stand,
  Let my People go.
  *Go down, Moses, way down in Egypt's
      land;*
  Tell old Pharaoh to let my People go.

2 The Lord told Moses what to do,
  Let my People go;
  To lead the children of Israel through,
  Let my People go.
  CHORUS

3 Your foes shall not before you stand,
  Let my People go;
  And you'll possess fair Canaan's land,
  Let my People go.
  CHORUS

4 O let us from all bondage flee,
  Let my People go;
  And let us all in Christ be free,
  Let my People go.
  CHORUS

5 I do believe without a doubt,
  Let my People go;
  That a Christian has a right to shout,
  Let my People go.
  CHORUS

Negro spiritual adapted
Peter D. Smith (1938–)

158 PEOPLE MATTER

1 Sing we of the modern city,
  Scene alike of joy and stress;
  Sing we of its nameless people
  In their urban wilderness.
  Into endless rows of houses
  Life is set a million-fold,
  Life expressed in human beings
  Daily born and growing old.

2 In the city full of people,
  World of speed and hectic days;
  In the ever-changing setting
  Of the latest trend and craze,
  Christ is present, and among us,
  In the crowd, we see him stand.
  In the bustle of the city
  Jesus Christ is every man.

3 God is not remote in heaven
  But on earth to share our shame;
  Changing graph and mass and numbers
  Into persons with a name.
  Christ has shown, beyond statistics,
  Human life with glory crowned;
  By his timeless presence proving
  People matter, people count!

Fred Kaan (1929–)

159 OUR CITY IS GOD'S CITY

1 All who love and serve your city,
  All who bear its daily stress,
  All who cry for peace and justice,
  All who curse and all who bless.

2 In your day of loss and sorrow,
  In your day of helpless strife,
  Honour, peace and love retreating,
  Seek the Lord, who is your life.

3 In your day of wealth and plenty,
  Wasted work and wasted play,
  Call to mind the word of Jesus,
  'Work ye yet while it is day.'

4 For all days are days of judgement,
  And the Lord is waiting still,
  Drawing near to men who spurn him,
  Offering peace from Calvary's hill.

5 Risen Lord, shall yet the city
  Be the city of despair?
  Come today, our Judge, our Glory,
  Be its name, 'The Lord is there!'

Erik Routley (1917–)

160 CHRIST THE WORKER

1 Christ the worker,
  Christ the worker,
  Born in Bethlehem,
  Born to work and die
  For every man.

2 Blessed man-child,
  Blessed man-child,
  Boy of Nazareth,
  Grew in wisdom as
  He grew in skill.

3 Skilful craftsman,
  Skilful craftsman,
  Blessed craftsman,
  Praising God by labour
  At his bench.

4 Yoke maker,
  Yoke maker,
  Fashioned by his hands,
  Easy yokes that made
  The labour less.

5 You who labour,
  You who labour,
  Listen to his call,
  He will make that heavy
  Burden light.

6 Heavy laden,
  Heavy laden,
  Gladly come to him,
  He will ease your load
  And give you rest.

7 Christ the worker,
  Christ the worker,
  Love alive for us,
  Teach us how to do
  All work for God.

*African hymn, collected Tom Colvin
(1925–)*

161 GOD'S PEACE

1 We pray for peace,
But not the easy peace
Built, not upon God's truth
But on complacency;
We pray for real peace,
The peace that love alone can seal.

2 We pray for peace,
But not the cruel peace,
Leaving our fellow men
To die in their distress;
We pray for real peace
Enriching all humanity.

3 We pray for peace,
And not the evil peace,
Defending unjust laws
And nursing prejudice,
But for the real peace
Of justice, truth and brotherhood.

4 We pray for peace
And, for that real peace,
We take our stand with Christ
To share his sacrifice,
Prepared to die for peace
And for its sake to forfeit it.

5 God give us peace;
If you withdraw your love
There is no peace for us
Nor any hope of it.
With you to lead us on,
Through death or tumult, peace will come.

Alan Gaunt (1935–)

162 THE DISGUISES OF CHRIST

1 We meet you, O Christ, in many a guise:
Your image we see is simple and wise.
You live in a palace, exist in a shack.
We see you, the gardener, a tree on your
back.

2 In millions alive, away and abroad;
Involved in our life you live down the
road.
Imprisoned in systems you long to be free.
We see you, Lord Jesus, still bearing your
Tree.

3 We hear you, O Man, in agony cry.
For freedom you march, in riots you die.
Your face in the papers we read and we
see.
The tree must be planted by human
decree.

4 You choose to be made at one with the
earth;
The dark of the grave prepared for your
birth.
Your death is your rising, creative your
Word;
The tree springs to life and our hope is
restored.

Fred Kaan (1929–)

163 HUMAN RIGHTS

1 For the healing of the nations,
Lord, we pray with one accord;
For a just and equal sharing
Of the things that earth affords.
To a life of love in action
Help us rise and pledge our word.

2 Lead us, Father, into freedom,
From despair your world release;
That, redeemed from war and hatred,
Men may come and go in peace.
Show us how through care and goodness
Fear will die and hope increase.

3 All that kills abundant living,
Let it from the earth be banned;
Pride of status, race or schooling,
Dogmas keeping man from man.
In our common quest for justice
May we hallow life's brief span.

4 You, Creator-God, have written
Your great name on all mankind;
For our growing in your likeness
Bring the life of Christ to mind;
That by our response and service
Earth its destiny may find.

Fred Kaan (1929–)

164 SHALOM

Shalom my friend,
God's peace, my friend,
Go with you now;
And stay with you
In all you do.
Shalom! Shalom!

Traditional

PROMISE

AND

FULFILMENT

in which we celebrate the Lordship of Christ and look forward to the completion of his purpose.

Recommended hymns from standard books

165 LIFE AND IMMORTALITY

1 O Lord of every shining constellation
  That wheels in splendour through the
      midnight sky:
  Grant us your Spirit's true illumination
  To read the secrets of your work on high.

2 You, Lord, have made the atom's hidden
      forces,
  Your laws its mighty energies fulfil;
  Teach us, to whom you give such rich
      resources,
  In all we use, to serve your holy will.

3 O Life, awaking life in cell and tissue,
  From flower to bird, from beast to brain
      of man;
  Help us to trace, from birth to final issue,
  The sure unfolding of your age-long plan.

4 You, Lord, have stamped your image on
      your creatures,
  And though they mar that image, love
      them still;
  Lift up your eyes to Christ, that in his
      features
  We may discern the beauty of your will.

5 Great Lord of nature, shaping and
      renewing,
  You made us more than nature's sons to
      be:
  You help us tread, with grace our souls
      enduing,
  The road to life and immortality.

A.F. Bayly (1901–)

166 GOD IS UNIQUE

1 God is unique and one—
  Father, Sustainer, Lord!
  Patterns of life were spun
  By his creative Word.
  Of his intention, love and care
  We are with growing trust aware.

2 Love came to earth in Christ,
  Man's common life to share;
  Choosing to be the least,
  Willing a cross to bear.
  He died, he rose, that we might live
  And all our love, responding, give.

3 The Holy Spirit moves
  Man to discover man;
  His inspiration proves
  More than the mind can span.
  Each listening heart is led to find
  The will of God for all mankind.

4 He shall forever reign,
  Ruler of time and space;
  God in the midst of men,
  Seen in the human face.
  We give expression to our creed
  By love in thought, in word and deed.

Fred Kaan (1929–)

167 TRANSFIGURING HOPE

1 Where there is darkness, let there be
    loving,
  Where there is doubting, let there be joy;
  Cry 'Hosanna', shout 'Hallelujah',
  Turn a world of hunger into a harvest of
    hope.

2 Where there is sickness, let there be
    healing,
  Where there is dying, let there be faith;
  Cry 'Hosanna', shout 'Hallelujah',
  Turn a world of grieving into a promise of
    hope.

3 Where there is anger, let there be justice,
  Where there is discord, let there be peace;
  Cry 'Hosanna', shout 'Hallelujah',
  Turn a world of chaos into a commune of
    hope.

4 Where there is squalor, let there be beauty,
  Where there is sadness, let there be light;
  Cry 'Hosanna', shout 'Hallelujah',
  Turn a world of strangers into the family
    of hope.

5 Where there is warfare, let there be
    judgement,
  Where there is suffering, let there be wrath;
  Cry 'Hosanna', shout 'Hallelujah',
  Turn the whole creation into transfiguring
    hope.

*Lucy Griffiths (1931–) and Brian Frost
(1935–)*

168 CLAIM HIS POWER

1 The world I walk in, rock and tree,
  Bird in the branches, fish in the sea,
  Created good, by man's default
  Surrendered to sin's assault.

2 So Christ his glory laid away,
  Bone of our bone he entered the fray,
  To captive man he brought release
  And flooded the world with peace.

3 The fight's still on and hearts must break,
  Justice and brotherhood are at stake;
  But we who're born to match this hour
  Step forward and claim his power.

4 The world I know is minted new,
  Everything crooked turned to the true:
  So as I go I'll dance and sing,
  'He's master of everything!'

Ian M. Fraser (1917–)

169 THE FIRST AND FINAL WORD

1 God who spoke in the beginning,
  Forming rock and shaping spar,
  Set all life and growth in motion,
  Earthly world and distant star;
  He who calls the earth to order
  Is the ground of what we are.

2 God who spoke through men and nations,
  Through events long past and gone,
  Showing still today his purpose,
  Speaks supremely through his Son;
  He who calls the earth to order
  Gives his word and it is done.

3 God whose speech becomes incarnate
  – Christ is servant, Christ is Lord! –
  Calls us to a life of service,
  Heart and will to action stirred;
  He who uses man's obedience
  Has the first and final word.

Fred Kaan (1929–)

170 A PRAYER FOR FULFILMENT

1 Lord, bring the day to pass
  When forest, rock and hill,
  The beasts, the birds, the grass,
  Will know your finished will:
  When man attains his destiny
  And nature its lost unity.

2 Forgive our careless use
  Of water, ore and soil —
  The plenty we abuse
  Supplied by other's toil:
  Save us from making self our creed,
  Turn us towards our brother's need.

3 Give us, when we release
  Creation's secret powers,
  To harness them for peace,
  Our children's peace and ours:
  Teach us the art of mastering
  Which makes life rich and draws death's
    sting.

4 Creation groans, travails,
  Futile its present plight,
  Bound — till the hour it hails
  The newfound sons of light
  Who enter on their true estate.
  Come, Lord: new heavens and earth
    create.

Ian M. Fraser (1917–)

171 BRIDGEBUILDING

Bridge a river, span a gorge,
Forge new ways ahead,
Reach another, find a brother,
Sister, lover, friend.
Cross the bridge and build with Christ
The New World he began,
Where people live together
In the family of man.

1 Colours decorate the world
  With shades of every hue,
  Human skins are black and brown,
  Pink and yellow too.
  Jumbled up together
  That's how they're to be seen,
  Keep them separated
  And the New World cannot be.
  CHORUS

2 Streams and rivers intertwine
  In their journey to the sea,
  People travel different routes
  To God and liberty;
  There is no room for prejudice
  In seekers after truth,
  So all join hands and make a bridge,
  I'll swing along with you.
  CHORUS

3 To live in ease when others starve
  Can tear the world apart,
  Our neighbour's desolation
  Is a burden on God's heart;
  The world's resources must be shared —
  A bridge of care be built
  Between the rich and poor folk
  So that all have food to eat.
  CHORUS

Peter Sharrocks (1940–)

172 CUT OUT TO BE WHAT?

1 Lord, I love to stamp and shout
  Testing lungs and muscles out;
  Other times I curl up still
  Dreaming till I've had my fill.

2 Lord, I love to watch things fly
  Whizzing, zooming, flashing by;
  Engines, aircraft, speedboats, cars,
  Spacecraft shooting to the stars.

3 Lord, I love to probe and pry
  Seeking out the reason why;
  Looking inside things and out
  Finding what they're all about.

4 Lord I'm many things and one
  Though my life's not long begun;
  You alone my secret see
  What I am cut out to be.

Ian M. Fraser (1917–)

173 WE MUST LEARN TO WAIT

1 Hurry up, clock!
   Can our friend be late?
   Yet it's still not time,
   And we have to wait.

2 Hurry up, time,
   To that party date!
   O how slow the days
   When we have to wait.

3 Hurry up, seed!
   But your growing rate,
   Just like ours, seems slow;
   We must learn to wait.

4 Hurry up, God!
   But the time will tell
   We can wait for you
   Knowing all is well.

Basil E. Bridge (1927–)

174 ALL RACES ARE ONE IN CHRIST

1 The God who rules this earth
   Gave life to every race;
   He chose its day of birth,
   The colour of its face;
   So none may claim superior grade
   Within the family he's made.

2 But sin infects us all,
   Distorts the common good;
   The universal fall
   Corrupts all brotherhood;
   So racial pride and colour strife
   Spread fear and hate throughout man's
      life.

3 Between the West and East,
   Yet neither black nor white,
   Behold! God's Son released!
   In whom all men unite.
   He comes with unrestricted grace
   To heal the hearts of every race.

4 That Man alone combines
   All lives within his own;
   That Man alone enshrines
   All flesh, all blood, all bone;
   That Man accepts all human pain,
   That Man breaks death, that Man shall
      reign.

5 To him we bring our praise,
   On him all hopes depend;
   Sole Master of our days,
   In him we see the End;
   Man's final Lord, God's perfect Son,
   In Jesus Christ are all made one.

Richard Jones (1926–)

175 THE KINGDOM HERE AND HEREAFT

1 Lord, in your Kingdom
   No sword is drawn,
   No sword is drawn
   But the sword of right,
   No sword is drawn
   But the sword of right.

2 Lord, in your Kingdom
   No strength is known,
   No strength is known
   But the strength of love,
   No strength is known
   But the strength of love.

3 Lord, in your Kingdom
   No fear can rise,
   No fear can rise
   But the fear of sin,
   No fear can rise
   But the fear of sin.

4 Lord, in your Kingdom
   No hate is found,
   No hate is found
   But the hate of wrong,
   No hate is found
   But the hate of wrong.

5 Lord, in your Kingdom
   No tears are shed,
   No tears are shed
   Save the tears of joy,
   No tears are shed
   Save the tears of joy.

Cyril G. Hambly (1931–)

176 THE TRIUMPHANT CHRIST

1 When the Lord in glory comes,
  Not the trumpets, not the drums,
  Not the anthem, not the psalm,
  Not the thunder, not the calm,
  Not the shout the heavens raise,
  Not the chorus, not the praise,
  Not the silences sublime,
  Not the sound of space and time,
  But his voice when he appears
  Shall be music to my ears —
  But his voice when he appears
  Shall be music to my ears.

2 When the Lord is seen again,
  Not the glories of his reign,
  Not the lightnings through the storm,
  Not the radiance of his form,
  Not his pomp and power alone,
  Not the splendours of his throne,
  Not his robe and diadems,
  Not the gold and not the gems,
  But his face upon my sight
  Shall be darkness into light —
  But his face upon my sight
  Shall be darkness into light.

3 When the Lord to human eyes
  Shall bestride our narrow skies,
  Not the child of humble birth,
  Not the carpenter of earth,
  Not the man by men denied,
  Not the victim crucified,
  But the God who died to save,
  But the victor of the grave,
  He it is to whom I fall,
  Jesus Christ, my All in all —
  He it is to whom I fall,
  Jesus Christ, my All in all.

Timothy Dudley-Smith (1926–)

177 THE FAMILY OF NATIONS

1 We turn to you, O God of every nation,
  Giver of life and origin of good;
  Your love is at the heart of all creation,
  Your hurt is people's broken brotherhood.

2 We turn to you, that we may be forgiven
  For crucifying Christ on earth again.
  We know that we have never wholly
    striven,
  Forgetting self, to love the other man.

3 Free every heart from pride and self-
    reliance,
  Our ways of thought inspire with simple
    grace;
  Break down among us barriers of defiance,
  Speak to the soul of all the human race.

4 On men who fight on earth for right
    relations
  We pray the light of love from hour to
    hour.
  Grant wisdom to the leaders of the nations,
  The gift of carefulness to those in power.

5 Teach us, good Lord, to serve the need of
    others,
  Help us to give and not to count the cost.
  Unite us all for we are born as brothers;
  Defeat our Babel with your Pentecost!

Fred Kaan (1929–)

INDEX OF FIRST LINES

(including First Lines of Choruses)

ACKNOWLEDGEMENTS

Copyright in the following items in this collection vest jointly in Stainer & Bell Ltd and the Methodist Church Division of Education and Youth, London: 13, 14, 19, 23, 24, 34, 35, 39, 52, 53, 54, 55, 59, 67, 68, 70, 75, 76, 77, 79, 90, 95, 107, 116, 118, 124, 126, 145, 146, 147, 155, 171, 173, 175.

Copies of copyright hymns may not be made without permission of the copyright owners, and enquiries about the hymns listed above should be addressed to Stainer & Bell Ltd, 82 High Road, London N2 9PW. For other copyright material, reference should be made to the person or company named below.

The Editors gratefully acknowledge permission to use copyright material as follows: Mr John Arlott for 17; Rev A.F. Bayly for 8 and 165; Peggy Blakeley and Don Harper and A & C Black Ltd for 18 (from 'Someone's Singing, Lord'); Bosworth & Co. Ltd, 14/18 Heddon Street, Regent Street, London W1R 8DP for 4 (copyright 1970 by Gustav Bosse Verlag, Regensburg, Germany, and assigned to Bosworth & Co. Ltd for British Commonwealth and USA; Mr G. Brattle for 115; Mr Tom Colvin for 160; Miss Margaret Cropper for 99; Rev Timothy Dudley-Smith for 2, 28, 94, 96, 117, 136 and 176; Miss E.W. Dunkerley for 138; B. Feldman & Co. Ltd, 138–140 Charing Cross Road, London WC2H 0LD for 177; Franciscan Communications Center, Los Angeles, Calif., USA 1975 for 108; David Higham Associates Ltd on behalf of the estate of the late Eleanor Farjeon for 7, from 'Children's Bells' published by Oxford University Press; Rev Richard Jones (copyright for USA reserved to Galaxy Music Corporation) for 153 and 174; Lorna Music Ltd for 149 © 1966; Mayhew McCrimmon Ltd, High Street, Great Wakering, Essex, for 133; Mayhew McCrimmon Ltd and Stainer & Bell Ltd for 128; Methodist Church Division of Education and Youth for 65; Methodist Publishing House for 119; Rev T.C. Micklem for 12; Moody Press, Moody Bible Institute of Chicago for 141, from 'Spirit of the Living God' © 1935, 1963; Rev Stephen Orchard for 135; Oxford University Press for 9 (from 'The Oxford Book of Carols'), 16, 26, 29, 30 (from 'Songs of Praise'), 32, 40, 44, 62, 80 (from 'Children Praising'), 81 (from 'The Oxford Book of Carols'), 83, 87, 91, 92, 105, 112, 113, 125, 134, 140 and 142; John Paul, The Preacher's Press for 84, 161; Rev K. Preston for 103; Society of the Sacred Mission for 104; Stainer & Bell Ltd for 1, 3, 6, 10, 11, 15, 20, 22, 27, 33, 36, 37, 38, 41, 42, 43, 45, 46, 47, 48, 49, 50, 51, 56, 58, 63, 64, 66, 69, 71, 72, 73, 74, 78, 82, 85, 86, 88, 89, 93, 97, 100, 101, 102, 106, 110, 114, 120, 121, 122, 123, 127, 129, 130, 132, 137, 139, 143, 150, 151, 152, 154, 156, 157, 158, 159, 162, 163, 166, 167, 168, 169, 170 and 172; Thank You Music for 144, © 1974; The Hymn Society of America for 21; Josef Weinberger Ltd, London, for 109, reprinted from the hymnbook 'Music for Series 3'.